ESSEC BUSINESS SCHOOL

MASTER IN HUMAN RESOURCES MANAGEMENT

Mastère Spécialisé en Management des Ressources Humaines - EMS RH 2011-2012

The Name of the Game

High-potentials identification and assessment: a comparative study of Talent Management Policies and Practices

Supervisor: Jean-Luc Cerdin

Lia Steindler

Promotion 2011-2012

Copyright © 2013 Lia Steindler
All rights reserved.

ISBN 10: 1481950290
ISBN 13: 9781481950299

INDEX

Acknowledgements v

Introduction ix

CHAPTER 1 – THE NAME OF THE GAME
Talent, High-potentials and stars: what do organization value?. 1
Individualization and its Limits. 7
Mindsets and Implicit beliefs. 14

CHAPTER 2 – THE NINE BOX GRID AND ITS IMPLICATIONS
Performance versus Potential: a logic fallacy 35
Non-Linear dynamics. 43
The Talent War and its implications. 52

CHAPTER 3 – COGNITIVE POTENTIAL: WHY WE WASTE TALENT
Cognitive Potential: Crystallized-And Fluid Intelligence. 67
Historical Background. 69
Crystallized Intelligence. 72
Fluid Intelligence (Gf). 78
Learning Agility 86

CHAPTER 4 – POTENTIAL WHAT FOR?
AN INTEGRATED MODEL
    High Potential qualities and traits 91
    The Foundational Dimension 105
    The Growth Dimension 114
    The ultimate sources of satisfaction 118

CHAPTER 5 – POTENTIAL IN DIFFERENT GAMES:
A COMPARATIVE STUDY
    Research Design and Methodology 125
    Research Methodology 126
    Research Philosophy and Inspiration 127
    Research Process 129
    Data analysis 131
    Field study results and findings 132
    Meaning of High potential and feelings about
    this subject 132
    Definitions : The What and the How of potential 137
    The grey-areas: how policies are applied 148
    To be or not to be? To tell or not to tell? 155
    Different models 172

CONCLUSION 185

APPENDIX 1 – Interview Guide 193

BIBLIOGRAPHY 197

Maurizio Cattelan's Horse (Untitled 2007) 212

Acknowledgements

First and foremost I would like to thank my supportive husband Guilherme, who has encouraged me throughout this project. I would also like to thank my family and friends for their patience and understanding, in particular my four children who have a mum who was often too busy.

Next I want to thank my interview partners in France, in the US and in the UK. They very kindly spent their valuable time, shared their experiences and reflections and allowed me to have an insight into talent management policies and practices. Without their commitment and openness, this study would not have been possible.

I would like to express my profound gratitude to my colleagues at Egon Zehnder who supported me throughout this project, in particular Daniel Tournier and Raymond Bassoulet who made this experience possible. A special thanks to Marc de Leyritz, Philippe Compagnon and Steve Kelner, who made themselves available, giving valuable advice and guidance. My sincerest gratitude to Irène Papaligouras for her insights, to Catherine Bousquet and Nancy Stone for their comments and reflections and all those patient souls who helped me accomplish this study.

Finally, I would like to thank Maurice Thévenet and Jean-Luc Cerdin for their time and guidance during this Master Degree in Human Resources Management at Essec Business School in Paris. This dissertation was defended on June 27TH 2012.

For Daniel, Adam, Ben and Clara

Introduction

In this dissertation, I would like to compare and discuss different talent management practices. The central issue of concern in this research is how organizations deal with their talent pool, and how, through different policies and practices, they manage to identify, develop and retain their outstanding employees, namely, in the terminology of the field, their high-potentials. High-potentials are considered the next generation of leaders. Over the past fifteen years the term high-potential became more frequent within large organizations: forty-two percent of twenty surveyed organizations in 1994 (Silzer, Slider & Knight, 1994) against one hundred percent in 2008 reported having a high-potential program (Silzer and Church, 2008). This tendency will be verified and we will compare and discuss how and why certain policies are introduced and the different ways they are applied.

The most common issue with high-potential in organizations is that, as a concept, it is poorly defined. The majority of the content regarding potential identification can primarily be drawn from three sources: trade press books from business schools, internal research from large organizations (not easy to access) and consulting firms. Competencies- and potential assessment are one of the core businesses of consulting firms, so that much of the research that does exist is centered on validating a specific assessment tool or model, and not on providing a comprehensive comparison of approaches to high-potentials' identification. The most common definition of potential is given in terms of vertical movement to a specific level in the organization within a given time span, meaning that an identified high-potential is supposed to step up two levels in a 2-5 years time span.

The idea for this research arose out of the necessity to find a clearer definition of high-potential and to identify a framework that allows for a better understanding of the qualities and traits we are looking for. This delineates the orientation of this research, namely to look into motivational theories in order to better understand one of the foundational aspects of potential: motivation. It is about having a better understanding and insight into what kind of goals we are after and why, as individuals and as an organization.

A first and most inspiring insight into potential, came from Carol S. Dweck publications, namely Implicit Theories (IPA: Implicit Personality Theories). *Implicit theories* are things we believe to be true. They can be defined as an individual's basic assumptions that provide a framework to guide our goals, they are the basis for what we use to approach new and old situations, make choices and decisions (Dweck, 1995).

According to Dweck (1995), there are mainly two types of implicit theorists - entity theorists and incremental theorists. The Entity theorists believe that traits are firmly established and fairly consistent, thus causing theorists to be confident in making assumptions from a minuscule amount of behavior; it's all about 'have' and 'have nots.' Incremental theorists believe traits are always varying over time; they can be developed. They see traits as not having much predictive value, and, therefore, are not as confident to pass judgments.

Entity and incremental views of traits form an important framework for understanding social judgments and biases, and in this particular case, they will be valuable in better understanding different potential identification and assessment practices. "Research on implicit theories is not to evaluate the "correctness' of people's beliefs because these theories are simply different ways of constructing reality" (Dweck, 1995). In this paper, implicit theories are used to show that having one view or the other can have meaningful consequences on what kind of potential we are looking for.

Learning agility is often cited in current literature as a key high-potential quality. We find, depending on the assessment model, other terms for cognitive selection criteria: cognitive agility, deriving insight, or learning flexibility. Cognitive ability is a central issue when it comes to identifying and selecting talent. I found, however, these terms poorly defined and described in an indistinct way. What is it that we are looking for when we speak of cognitive abilities or cognitive potential? I decided to consider recent theories in cognitive psychology and to see what kind of cognitive construct *learning agility* could be related to.

This theoretical background gave significant insights into the field study that included interviewing fifteen senior HR professionals from large listed organizations. The semi-structured interviews focused on their talent management policies and practices. A part of the questions focus on policies, meaning the official standpoint of the organizations about a specific topic, as for example to tell or not to tell high-potentials they are on the list. A second part of the interview guide focuses on practices, meaning disclosing what lies beneath policies and how official positions are applied. Finally, there are questions that focus on the personal standpoint of the interviewee, his/her personal views and feelings about a given policy or practice.

Outline

This dissertation is structured into five main chapters and begins with evaluating the existing literature on talent management versus high-potential management. It will discuss current definitions of talent and potential and the most common uses of these terms, in addition to how they have evolved in the literature. It will focus on potential identification and assessment. Trends related to talent management and high-potential management programs will be discussed. The **second** chapter focuses on recent literature in motivational psychology- as well as organizational behavior theories. The assumption is that these theories have important implications for certain talent management practices and choices. The **third** chapter discusses new findings in cognitive psychology that could lead to new assessment approaches related to some consistent or stable variables. It will provide an introduction to recent cognitive psychology theories currently discussed by researchers about the foundational- and the growth-dimension discussed above. The **fourth** chapter discusses high-potential qualities and traits, comparing different 'potential models'. This is followed by a **fifth** chapter that presents the research results of a semi-structured interview guideline with fifteen senior HR professionals working for large listed organizations (CAC 40, DAX 30, FTSE 500) in France, in the UK and in the USA. It compares the different approaches organizations choose in order to manage their key-talent, striving to achieve a talent management policy that supports sustained motivation and enables people to unleash their potential. The theories presented in the previous chapters are key to understanding the "best" possible approaches not in generic terms, but rather according to each company's values and needs. Finally, this study will conclude with a series of recommendations in light of the research findings, the discussed theories, as well as some personal reflections related to the experience of interviewing senior HR professionals.

The method is the key
The process
The beliefs
The culture
The leaders

Chapter 1

THE NAME OF THE GAME

TALENT, HIGH-POTENTIALS AND STARS: WHAT DO ORGANIZATIONS VALUE?

The term Talent can be used in different contexts and can have different meanings. Maurice Thévenet in his recent publication (2008) gives us an interesting insight into how its connotations have changed over time. Talent has often been associated with particular competencies, be it in a given professional sector, the arts, or arts and crafts. We find the term talent also in career management literature as a special endowment which is not immediately effective, but rather a promise of future endowment. Others, like Boudreau and Ramstad (2007) associate the term with either personal or collective competencies. Since the article "The War for Talent" (1997) was published, it's not clear whether the term talent is associated with specific competencies or in general to people. Where the term refers to people we tend to speak of high-potentials or highly talented professionals or experts. In many organizations Talent and High-potential became synonyms (O'Toole and Lawler, 2006), meaning that those people are capable to developing competencies and occupying higher

The Name of the Game

positions in terms of scope and responsibility in the future. Thévenet did a research on how HR professionals describe or define this category. He identified three contexts the term talent can be associated with: the first refers to personal competencies that are absolutely unique and do not enter into what we can call general or classical competencies or skills (so original and associated to a particular person that it's impossible to apply them to a general talent pool); the second refers to people who are particularly talented (representing normally less than 5% of the total population of the company); the third, is more of a developmental approach to talent, not perceived as an endowment, a stable trait, but much more as an acquired competency or skill that must be developed, whatever the initial level it would need constant effort and work to be improved. Thévenet affirms that the different use of the term talent actually reveals five different phenomena. The one that really marks a quite recent tendency is a shift towards individualization practices within human resources management. According to A.Roger and D.Boullier "Talents are seen as a sub-set of skills; those in which the person concerned excels, and which distinguish them from others" ("Talents et potentiels" in J.M. Peretti *Tous talentuex, 2009*). This kind of pseudo-definition always strikes me, since they create the illusion of clarifying something, leaving what we actually know (or rather do not know) unchanged. What are the so called sub-set of skills? Are they specific competencies? Are they derived from experience? Are they natural, innate capabilities? Thévenet distinguishes competence from talent and talent from potential in these terms: "Competence is a collective concept that involves every individual in the company, whereas talent refers only to those who are different and who deliver a high level of added value. Competence can be measured and calibrated against a scale, whereas talent expresses itself in terms of the unique nature of the outcome achieve. Talent is often compared with potential: potential refers to the future and probability, whilst talent is a present reality. Talent is proven potential." (C. Dejoux and M.Thévenet 2012). Talent[1] presumes that there are rare skills, the attainment of exceptional results and a leadership style from which the individual draws his or her exceptional motivation, write Dejoux and Thévenet. Motivation and leadership styles are presented as strongly related, my interpretation is that leadership styles actually can strongly differ depending on what kind of motivation *moves* us, i.e. power motivation, growth and learning motivation, need of validation etc. An interesting talent model the authors present rests on three concepts which interact with each other and apply equally to individuals, groups and companies : competence, performance, leadership.

This model applies to most talent management practices. Recently however a new talent and high-potential profile has emerged, that does not include as a pre-condition "leadership skills". It's the so called "expert" profile. In highly

---

1 Ulrich, D., *The talent trifecta. Workforce Management* , Sept. 2006, pp.32–33. This present day HR guru defines talent in terms of: .talent=competenceXcommitmentXcontribution (Ulrich, 2006). In his formulation, competence means that individuals have the knowledge, skills and values that are required for today and tomorrow. Commitment means that employees work hard, put the time in to do what they are asked to do, giving their discretionary energy to the firm's success. Contribution means that they are making a real contribution through their work — finding meaning and purpose in their work.

complex sectors, like the nuclear sector, there are skills and competencies that are rare and vital for the business. Those profiles don't necessarily need leadership motivation or leadership skills to be considered key- talent. What we can perceive however is a tendency towards individualization since the late 1990s. Thévenet and Dejoux presented an overview of the evolution of the HR function towards talent management that gives an interesting insight of past and present trends:

	TAYLORI-AN MODEL	FLEXIBILI-TY MODEL	GPEC MODEL (gestion prévision-nelle)	TALENT MODEL
	1870-1970	1970-1990	1990-2000	2000-
PRINCIPLES	Do everything yourself	Multi-task	Adapt and suggest	Promote your rare skills
ORGANIZATION	Pyramidal	Matrix	Cellular	Global
	Personnel Administration	HR Management	HR-Business Partner	Talent-Business Integrator
CAREERS	Hierarchical promotion	Accumulation of specialties	Job-cross functionality	Voluntary mobility
	Carrer mgmt. by the employer	Mobility supported by employer	Multiple employers	Career-self-management with support from employer
TOOLS	Pay classification	Career Management Recruitment Training	Skills development tools benchmarking annual appraisal mapping	Succession planning, training with focus on emotional intelligence skills and leadership skills, coaching and mentoring

(Talent Management, 2012, p.102)

These are general trends that have been observed during the past decades and give a picture of how models have evolved. However, there are companies that are still stuck in what has been called the flexibility model (1970-1990). In this model, HR tools are basically limited to career management determined by seniority. The setup of a job and competency planning solution (GPEC) model refers to the benchmark of skills and refers to McClelland's competency/performance approach that will be discussed further on. The current trend is a talent-business integrated approach. In this approach the reference is training in emotional intelligence skills through coaching and mentoring, developing leadership skills, and the focus is clearly a "succession planning" focus. There are further tools, such as the nine-box grid, which was derived from the GPEC model (1990-2000) and has been adapted by some organizations to current needs as we will see in the next chapter.

Thévenet and Dejoux give also an interesting overview of Talent Management success factors and associated key-processes (Thévenet and Dejoux 2012, p.104):

The Name of the Game

ATTRACT
- Develop an attractive employer market branding communication
- Identify talented people internally for development
- Analyse current and future needs in terms of talent

RECRUIT
- Make talent part of social responsibility policy
- Practice continual recruitment
- Develop new arguments for Generation Y

RETAIN
- Understand motivation factors
- Turn managers and senior into talent developers
- Invest in high quality working conditions and ongoing recognition

DEVELOP
- Take interest in the individual
- Widespread implementation of development tools
- Set the required level of responsibility and results
- Continual evaluation and training
- Manage conflict
- Teach self-esteem

RECOGNISE
• Instigate a culture of success • Rethink succession planning • Remunerate talented people • Promote exceptional performance
COMPARE BEST PRACTICES/ BENCHMARKING

Some of these themes will be discussed in the following chapters, with the main focus on *retain, develop and recognize* and the fifth chapter is dedicated to a **comparative analysis**.

INDIVIDUALIZATION AND ITS LIMITS

The assumption is: wherever you put them they will continue being stars. They will succeed and over-perform. However, if we look at studies that analyzed how stars performed and were able to adjust to new organizations, we will see that in most cases they weren't able to perform as they did in the past. They were stars in organization A and moving to organization B they seldom achieved the same level of performance as they had before. Sometimes they managed to over-perform only after 2-3 years in the new organization, sometimes they never managed to achieve the same level of performance. This means that there is a general tendency to underestimate the importance and impact of the company's environment, the importance of having a strong and effective internal network, the fact of being known internally and sometimes having access to senior management support and mentoring, access to tools

The Name of the Game

and processes that give a framework and structure in addition to the practical means and budgets that are put at employees' disposal. Those aspects contribute greatly to becoming a shining star or, in their absence, to becoming a falling star, as the title of Maurice Thévenet's book implies : *"Des étoiles brillantes aux étoiles…filantes"* (2008). Another article which appeared in the Harvard Buisiness Review ten years earlier was entitled *"The risky business of hiring Stars (Groysberg, B.; Nanda, A.; Nohria, N.; HBR may 2004)*. The first sentences of this second article make explicit reference to "the war for talent". We can trace the beginning of this individualization process within organizational behavior and talent management processes to the eighties, however it's in the late nineties, with the use of the term "talent war", that we can see a clear "dramatization" of this tendency. The fact of talking about a war for talent and of CEO's leading their talent war "down in the trenches" in order "to battle for the best and brightest people" provides a hint of what I meant by dramatizing and heading towards individualization. In this article they carried out a study of A players, stars in a given organization and measured their performance when they were recruited by another organization to check whether they still lived up to expectations. They observed that top performers in all those groups were more like comets than stars. They were blazing successes for a while, but quickly faded out when they left one company for another. It wasn't clear why stars were unable to extend their achievements across companies. Within the Financial Services sector over 1000 star stock analysts who worked in various investment banks in the United States over a period of 9 years (until 1996) were studied. For purposes of the study, they defined 'star' as any analyst who was ranked by Institutional Investor magazine as one of the best in the industry in any of those nine years. The findings were surprising, to say the least. When a company hires a star, the star's performance plunges, there is a sharp decline in the functioning of the group or team the person works with, and the company market value falls. Moreover, they found that stars don't stay with organizations for long, despite the astronomical salaries firms lure them away from rivals and retain them. Once they are labeled stars it's very difficult for them to accept setback and failure. If they don't work as well in the new organization as they did in the past, they tend to attribute failure and the plunge in performance not to themselves, but to the new context, the new organization, or anyone except themselves. We will see later on why this is the case. In this article Groysberg et al. showed that 46% of the research analysts did poorly in the year after they left one company for another. After they switched, their performance plummeted by an average of about 20% and, what is even more surprising, is that they had not climbed back to old levels even 5 years later. So, we can conclude that decline in a star's performance was more or less permanent. Furthermore, Groysberg and al. observed that once stars start changing jobs, they keep moving to the highest bidders, instead of allowing employers to build businesses around them. We can speak of an individualization tendency within organizations, but also of an 'individualist trend'. Obviously a highly talented professional doesn't suddenly become less intelligent or lose a decade of work experience overnight when he/she switches firms. However, most companies overlook this

The Name of the Game

fact: an executive's performance depends on both his/her personal competencies and capabilities and the organization's resources, such as the systems and processes of the organization he/she works for. When the employee leaves, he cannot take the firm-specific resources that contributed to the achievements. As a result, this person is unable to repeat his performance. As the authors put it, there is another aspect that should not be under-estimated: equity (Adams, 1963). "Resentful of the rainmaker (and his pay), other managers avoid the newcomer, cut off information to him, and refuse to cooperate. That hurts the star's ego as well as his ability to perform". The arrival of a star, of a highflyer, often results in interpersonal conflicts and a breakdown of communication within the group. As a result, the group's performance, not only the newcomer's performance, suffers for several years. Hiring stars can profoundly impact motivation. Scott Adams represents this kind of situation:

DILBERT © (2009) Scott Adams. Used By permission of UNIVERSAL UCLICK. All rights reserved.

Groysberg and al. report an interview with a head of research department at an investment bank who stated that hiring stars resembles an organ transplant: "First, the new body can reject the prized organ that operated so well inside another body... on some occasions, the new organ hurts healthy parts of the body by demanding a disproportionate blood supply... other parts of the body start to resent it, ache, and demand attention...or threaten to stop working. You should think about it very carefully before you do a (transplant) to a healthy body. You could get lucky, but success is rare". The study showed that team moves, teams of research analysts, salespeople and traders performed better than analysts who moved solo. Thus, the company is a large part of the reason why stars become and stay stars. The authors focus on the individual factors that contribute to performance: innate abilities, education (including professional training) experience and competencies. It's not clear which abilities or traits the authors refer to, when they speak of innate abilities. This is an example of implicit theories, they don't specify the framework, what they believe is fixed, and what they believe is developmental. In the third chapter the innate abilities versus the acquired abilities will be discussed : fluid versus crystallized intelligence. Paradoxically it's the crystallized intelligence people will be always able to develop. Talent involves both fluid and crystallized intelligence, however environment conditions are key. Most companies underestimate the degree to which a star's success depends on the following company-specific factors : Company's resources and capabilities (company's reputation, financial means and its human *resources*) that enabled the employee to do the things that really mattered; Systems and Processes that give a framework and procedures that contribute to the individual's success; Leadership, meaning that in most companies bosses give talented employees the resources and

The Name of the Game

support they need to become stars. The authors noticed that it was impossible for analysts to survive without supportive supervisors. Between 1990 and 1992, when Lehman Brothers' equity research department was the best on Wall Street, its star analysts attributed their success in large part to the direction and guidance provided by their bosses Jack Rivkin and Fred Fraenkel. That was still a few years before toxic assets made their appearance and determined the downfall of this investment bank. That's why besides these organization's aspects the authors name, including internal networks and training, the importance of personality traits as emotional and social intelligence should not be underestimated (Goleman, D. 2000, Goleman,D.; Boyatzis, R.; McKee, A. 2002, Goleman, D. 2011) as well as the leader's role in creating a climate that supports healthy relationships and a positive focus on the future (Zander Stone, R.; Zander B. 2000 Harvard Buisness School Press). An interesting concept developed by Cerdin (2004) is "360°degree support", an analogy to the 360°-degree feedback approach used in performance appraisal, which states that individuals may not only rely on themselves in building their careers, but may, and need to, look for the support of others, including their supervisors, peers, mentors and network, including of course their family. This is possible in the case where there is a good supervisor. We will see later on how bad bosses can be profoundly toxic and bring about a decrease in cognitive abilities that seriously impact performance. That's why Groysberg and al. strongly support the practice of growing talent within the organization and doing everything possible to retain the stars they create. We see this policy in many organizations, such as

THE NAME OF THE GAME

Procter & Gamble, GE, L'Oréal, Johnson&Johnson, Unilever, Coca-Cola, Schlumberger and many others. Some of them are thought of as Human Resources best practices, they know that homegrown stars tend to outperform imported stars, besides the fact that they are also more loyal. These companies don't exclude external hiring, but focus mostly on their resources and on growing talent. Groysberg and al. noted that there are some exceptions. Companies that not only managed to retain talent they created, but who were also able to absorb stars when they did hire them. They noted that there are usually three people-development philosophies among organizations. Most firms hire hardworking people, don't do much to develop them, but focus on retaining the high-level stars they bring from outside. Other companies recruit smart people and develop some into stars, knowing that they may lose them to rivals. Only a few corporations recruit bright people, develop them into stars, and do everything possible to retain them. *"Any of these approaches may let a team win the World Series once, but in business, the only viable strategy is to recruit good people, develop them and retain as many of the stars as possible. That sounds tough, but it isn't impossible, as companies like Lehman Brothers and Goldman Sachs did in the 1990s. They did not use fancy tricks or shortcuts to develop stars; they were patient about the way they chose people and painstakingly trained them to excel."* (Harvard Business Review, Groysberg and al. 2004). An aspect that should not be ignored is the reason behind the choice of hiring stars. An organization might have made this choice to bring on board people that were expected to develop new business, or to replace employees who left or to strengthen existing teams. The study reports that the stars whose performance declined the most were those who had been hired to establish new businesses or strengthen teams. The authors believe that the former failed because there were few complementary capabilities they could use, while the latter had to fight the system – that is, the existing team. What they mean by "few complementary capabilities" is not clear and they do not enter into further detail. However in my point of view it is a key aspect that should be further investigated and that I will refer to later on in this paper in the second and third chapter. Developing new business means taking a chance and facing a high probability of failure. Why should a star, who knows he/she is a star, take any risks? Why should someone who's been labeled a star expose himself to possible setbacks?

MINDSETS AND IMPLICIT BELIEFS

There is no doubt that some people are more talented than others. There are certainly naturally talented people who have special endowments in one particular field rather than another. Nevertheless, talent in a "fixed mindset" can lead to setback and failure. Carol S. Dweck shows the power of people's beliefs. Our beliefs about our abilities influence what we think is possible – and what we might be able to achieve. Interestingly, it's not just whether or not you think you have ability that matters. In fact, what seems to be most important is whether or not you think you can get ability. In other words, do you think that intelligence (or personality, self-efficacy or athletic power) is something that is fixed, or something that is malleable? Psychologists call these beliefs implicit theories

THE NAME OF THE GAME

"they are personal beliefs about the kind of thing intelligence is (personality, or morality, or any other kind of characteristic or quality). They are called *implicit* because they aren't necessarily something you have thought consciously or deliberately about. But despite the fact that we may not even realize that we hold them, these theories are powerful shapers of the choices we make for ourselves every day" (Heidi Grant Halvorson, 2011).

As described by Grant Halvorson, these beliefs we are aware of or unaware of affect our choices, as well as what we want and whether we succeed in attaining it. One of the pioneers of implicit theories is Albert Bandura ("Organizational Applications of Social Cognitive Theory", 1988) and in his work he shows how relevant this topic is when discussing talent and in particular potential. Albert Bandura, the Stanford University psychologist who pioneered the study of self-efficacy, points out the contrast between those who doubt themselves and those who believe in their abilities when it comes to taking on a difficult task. Those with self-efficacy gladly step up to the challenge, those with self-doubt don't even try, regardless of how well they might actually do. Self-confidence raises aspirations and what was striking in one of his well-known *mindset* studies is that the level of self-efficacy was a stronger predictor of job performance than the actual level of skill or training the 112 accountants who underwent this study had received before being hired (in D. Goleman, 2000). Dweck went a step further. Her work aims at showing how changing people's beliefs – even the simplest beliefs – can have profound effects. In her book *Mindsets (2007)*, she explains how a simple belief about oneself – a belief she and her researchers discovered

The Name of the Game

in their research and tests – guide a large part of our lives. Much of what we think of as our personality actually grows out of this "mindset". Much of what might be preventing you from fulfilling your potential grows out of it or depends on it. What is interesting is to understand *how* Dweck arrived at these discoveries. She was obsessed with understanding how people cope with failures and setbacks. She started observing how students deal with difficult problems. She noticed with great surprise that some students confronted with hard puzzles, instead of looking crestfallen, rubbed their hands together and cried out "I love a challenge!" Her assumption was that either you know how to cope with failure or you don't. She had never thought that anyone would love being exposed to possible failure. She figured out that those children knew something she didn't. Dweck's aim became to understand what kind of "mindset" could turn failure into a gift. What did they know those children? They knew that human skills and qualities could be cultivated through effort. Not only were they not discouraged or depressed by setback, they did not event think they were failing. They thought they were *learning*. Many of us think that human qualities are carved in stone. You are smart, intelligent, gifted, naturally endowed or you aren't. Dweck shows throughout her experiments the consequences of thinking that our intelligence or personality are something you can develop, as opposed to something that is fixed, a deep-seated trait. She reports her personal experiences and remembers how her teacher in the early sixties asked the students to be seated around the room in IQ order, meaning that they were seated according to their IQ scores.

THE NAME OF THE GAME

Unlike Binet, this teacher believed that people's IQ scores were immutable and that they told the whole story of who they were. Binet when elaborating a measure for cognitive intelligence had a different goal. He designed this test to identify children who were not profiting from French Public schooling in the early twentieth century, so that new and more effective educational programs could be designed to get them back on track. Without denying individual differences in children's intellects, he believed that education and practice and new strategies could bring about fundamental changes in intelligence (crystallized intelligence as we will discuss later). Unfortunately this part of his legacy has been often ignored. We can quote a few lines of Binet's book *Modern ideas about children* in which he summarizes his research on hundreds of children with learning difficulties: "*A few modern philosophers…assert that an individual's intelligence is a fixed quantity, a quantity which cannot be increased. We must protest and react against this brutal pessimism… With practice, training, and above all, method, we manage to increase our attention, our memory, our judgment and literally to become more intelligent than we were before*". Today most experts sustain that it's not an either – or situation. It's not 100% nature or 100% nurture, nor either genes versus environment, nor inborn versus acquired. Gilbert Gottlieb, an eminent neuroscientist affirms that not only do genes and environment cooperate as we develop, but genes require input from the environment to work properly. This might give us another reading of the study carried out by Groysberg and al. (1998) mentioned above, on those young stars that managed to adapt and over-perform in

The Name of the Game

new organizations and those who did not. Many companies don't realize that their human resources philosophy, their approach to talent management, dictates how successful – or unsuccessful – they are at developing stars, motivating or de-motivating homegrown talent and integrating hired stars. Scientists are learning that people have more capacity for lifelong learning and brain development than they ever thought possible.

In the study of careers (J.L.Cerdin, A.Bird 2004) there can be two possible paradigms, one that can be defined as a universalist approach, and the other a contextual paradigm. The universalist approach gives rise to the notion of a "best practice" and encourages a search for a 'best way', whereas the contextual paradigm focuses on the unique features of institutional environment, including the legal and the cultural environments, which give rise to distinctive, environment-specific practices (J.L.Cerdin, A. Bird 2004, p.207). The concept, for example, of "career potential" can vary across countries and cultures and has relevant implications for what defines potential and how and when it should be identified. More specifically four models – the Japanese model, the Latin model, the Germanic model and the multinational corporation model- may serve as the basis for understanding how careers may be structured in different contexts. The very meaning of what is a career in terms of advancement in a given structure varies from context to context. High-potential in organizations is strictly related to career advancement, by its very definition, as we will discuss later on. The four models are:

- The Japanese model - also called 'elite cohort approach' depicts a career structure in which the identification of potential occurs at the time of initial recruitment followed by a long trial period of 7 to 8 years. Only the winners in this time-constrained tournament are given challenging responsibilities at each level of advancement within the organization.

- The Latin model – or 'elite political approach', of which France is a typical example, is an elitist and political process in which top leaders are selected, mainly from the 'Grandes Ecoles'. The elite moves along a path of cross-functional challenges.

- The German model places a premium on functional expertise and is fundamentally meritocratic since it praises acquired experience. Apprenticeships constitute trial periods, in order to identify individuals with potential who will climb up the functional ladder.

- The multinational corporation model is not based on elite recruitment in identifying potential, but rather on decentralized recruitment at the local subsidiary level. Local subsidiaries recruit not just for jobs but also for potential. The subsequent development of potential within the organizations is managed at corporate level with no preferences given to any nationality.

As Cerdin and Evans (Evans et al, 2002) commented, the first three models have come increasingly under pressure from progressive globalization. Furthermore, it is important to

The Name of the Game

notice, that these four models are structural, that is, careers are viewed as a "structural aspect of an organization"(Rosenbaum, 1993). As Cerdin indicates - and this is a key-issue, *"the structural model defines the rules of the game that operate in a given context"* (Cerdin, 2004) When the context changes, such as when an individual relocates to another country, or when a star moves to a new organization, the rules of the game, such as valuing diplomas or professional experiences -as well as mindsets-, also change. What might send a positive signal in one particular context, may not send any signal, or may send a negative signal, in another context. In this paper we will try to stick to the second paradigm, the contextual approach that aims at revealing the ambiguous aspects that lie behind the different "games" and give some contrast to the "grey-areas". Implicit theories are of great interest in this context, because they relate to and encompass both the viewpoint of the individual and the viewpoint of the organization. Both individual and organizational perspectives vary and tend to influence one another with regard to the way that talent issues are addressed and implemented. Robert Sternberg, one of the present-day gurus of intelligence, writes that the major factor in whether people achieve expertise and unleash their full potential "is not some fixed prior ability, but purposeful engagement". It's not always people who start out the smartest who end up the smartest. One of Dweck's experiments has been for me some sort of Copernican revolution. It shows that the view you adopt for yourself profoundly affects the way you lead your life. I will report her experiment because the procedure and the results are impressive. She formulated the idea that students could have different theories about their intelligence – it could be viewed as a fixed trait or as a malleable quality that could be developed. She then began to show that these theories of intelligence were the basis for the goals that students pursued and for their reactions to failure. Her first experiments culminated in a Psychological Review, an article Dweck wrote with Ellen Leggett showing how these "implicit theories" could shed light on basic processes of motivation and personality. Organizations keep testing, assessing IQ, personality traits and motivation in order to predict potential, however they ignore implicit theories. That's why Dweck and Leggett's studies are of particular interest. In *Subtle Linguistic Cues Affect Children's motivation (Dweck,C.; Cimpian A., Ace, H.M., Markman, E.; 2007)*, and other experiments applied to graduate students and professionals that yielded similar results, they tested reactions to a setback. They verified how people reacted to a setback depending on whether their successes were rewarded by generic or non-generic praise. As an example of generic praise we can say "John is friendly", since it reports a general regularity, a stable trait. In contrast, the non-generic "John was friendly at the party" refers to a specific event, a given context in the past. Generic sentences about an individual imply that the particular behavior commented on - "John is intelligent" – stems from a stable trait or skill (Gelman & Heyman, 1999). Are people sensitive to this subtle connotation with respect to their own behavior? If so, then generic praise may lead children as well as adults to think in fixed trait terms (a label), meaning that later mistakes could signal a negative trait of low ability and therefore undermine motivation (Dweck, 1999, 2006). Her

The Name of the Game

study supports the fact that praising a whole person (e.g. "you are a good girl/boy", "you are amazingly smart") after success on a given task, fostered helpless responses to subsequent mistakes, as opposed to praising the process through which success was achieved (e.g. "You found a good way to solve it" or "I must have put in a lot of effort to get there").

Surprisingly she notes that motivation does not increase with increased levels of praise, instead rather it tends to dip. When we label our talented employees 'high-potentials' communicating formally and praising their status, are we sure we are increasing their motivation? If asked, high potentials might answer that it does, but research would seem to prove the contrary, especially if facing a setback situation. Dweck's research casts some light on how our minds work, how we react to different stimuli.

Another experiment Dweck performed showed the possible negative consequences of generic praise. She gave every child a test that consisted of fairly easy puzzles. The researcher informed all the children of their scores, adding a single six-word sentence of praise. Half the kids were praised for their intelligence i.e. *you must be smart at this*, and half were praised for their effort i.e. *you must have worked really hard*. The children were tested a second time, but this time were offered a choice between a harder test and an easier test. Ninety percent of the kids who'd been praised for their effort chose the harder test. A majority of the kids who'd been praised for their intelligence, on the other hand, chose the easy test. Why? "*When we praise children for their intelligence,*" Dweck wrote, "*we tell them that's the name of the game : look smart, don't risk making mistakes*". The third level of tests was uniformly harder; none of the kids did well. However, the two groups of kids reacted very differently to the situation. The praised-for-effort group tried all possible solutions, testing different strategies to the puzzles and said "they liked it" wrote Dweck. But the group praised-for-intelligence hated the harder test, they took it as proof they weren't smart. She finished the experiment by a last test of the same difficulty as the initial test. The praised-for-effort group improved their initial score by 30 percent, while the praised-for-intelligence group's score declined by 20 percent. Subtle linguistic cues affect motivation. Dweck was so surprised at the result of this experiment that she re-ran it five times. The result did not change. Dweck says that people are incredibly attuned to messages telling them what is valued *"We go around all the time looking, looking, trying to understand 'who am I in this setting? Who am I in this framework?'"* We react to what seem to be the expectations: to the name of the game.

In this case the game is called the high-potential game. By sending this message what are we expecting in terms of consequences and results? We should think carefully about what message we are giving and how we are communicating it, since it might make a big difference: subtle linguistic differences can be relevant. David Coyle (2009) confirms Dweck's studies: each of the talent hotbeds he visited used language that affirmed the value of effort and slow progress rather than innate talent or intelligence. What we can retain from Dweck's study is also that both generic and non-generic praise are equally rewarding. So, if we looked for an argument to support our choice concerning the best way of rewarding and thus retaining talent, we would

The Name of the Game

now deduce that giving generic praise, labeling, would not achieve this. Believing that your qualities are given and stable, carved in stone – the fixed mindset – creates an urgency to prove yourself over and over again. Children that were praised for intelligence –who were granted generic praise – were put into a box. The box contained those labeled intelligent, smart in general terms, not applied to a given context or task. This put the children into a fixed-mindset. Exposure to failure meant questioning their profound identity, failure meant they weren't smart. Every situation, in the fixed-mindset, calls for a confirmation of one's intelligence, personality or character. Every situation will be evaluated in terms of probability of succeeding or failing, looking smart or dumb, being accepted or rejected, feeling like a winner or a loser, being considered a winner or a loser. There is another option in which these traits are not simply cards you were dealt by destiny and you have to live with, "always trying to convince yourself and others that you have a royal flush when you're secretly worried it's a pair of tens. In growth-mindset the hand you are dealt is just the starting point for development" writes Dweck. This *growth mindset* is based on the belief that your basic qualities are things you can develop and cultivate through effort. Despite the different level of initial endowment in their initial talents and aptitudes, in the growth mindset everyone can change and grow through application and experience (Dweck 2007). This does not mean *everything*, like preferences or values, can be changed. When referring to values we will consider values and motives as a same concept. Many psychologists remain convinced that the distinction between values and motives is unnecessary and confusing (Raven, 1988). As we will discuss further on, a current reason for rejecting this distinction derives from the cognitive revolution in psychology, which shifted attention to conscious rather than unconscious motivation. Modern investigators have focused more on information processing and on the way in which motivational thoughts are converted into action. We can define values as "self-attributed motives or normative beliefs about desirable goals and modes to conduct" (McClelland et al., Psychological Review 1989, vol. 96, N°4). Motives will be one of the key subjects in the following chapters and are important when evaluating potential for a given position. If the organizations' policy is to put highly talented people into a "high-potential" box, what are the risks and possible consequences of this talent management policy? We will try to answer those questions throughout this paper by comparing different practices and policies elaborated to address the needs of the organization and of this talented population.

The endowed, the profile Carol Dweck would define as "natural" talent, is the one who needs a whole life to prove and testify the presence of a gift. Naturals are those that our culture unfortunately tends to consider highly, the effort-less success, the flawless and naturally bright. Those that prove to be flawless right away. If you have it you have it, if you don't you don't. Effort is often perceived as a deficiency, if you have to put in effort that means that you "don't have it". What could make someone a non-learner? Praising and valuing effortless success: the fixed mindset. Everyone is born with a strong drive to learn, babies stretch their skills daily. They never decide it's too hard to learn to talk or to walk or that's not worth the effort. Babies don't worry about making mistakes and starting all over again. The desire to think of yourself as perfect, as naturally endowed with gifts, is often called the CEO disease.

Heidi Grant Halvorson's research (2011) brought further insight into implicit beliefs theory. Basing her studies on Dweck's research, she focused on how beliefs can shape our tendency to focus on goals that are about **performance**, or goals that are about **progress**. When we assess talent and potential we should keep in mind these two kinds of goals and how they differ from one another. They differ in ways that *really* matter. As a social psychologist she spent years studying achievement, observing thousands of research participants pursue goals at work or in the classroom. Why do we fail to reach our goals? She noticed that most of the time people reported not having enough 'willpower', but surprisingly willpower is not what we think it is. What really makes the difference is self-control. Self-control appears to be the ability to guide your actions in pursuit of a goal – to persevere and stay on course, despite temptations, distractions, and the demands of competing goals. Another interesting point she makes is that self-control does not work the way you might think it does. Psychologists have come to understand that the capacity for self-control is very much like a muscle. Like a muscle self-control can vary from person to person, but also from moment to moment. Self-control is learned and developed and made stronger (or weaker) over time, it's neither innate nor unchangeable. When it comes to reaching a goal, countless times you might have heard "do your best". It is supposed to inspire you, but it doesn't. It's actually a lousy motivator. Primarily it's a lousy motivator because 'do your best' is very vague. It's so generic, that you don't know *what* it refers to, nor *how* to get there. In motivation as in praise, we should avoid being generic, as it's a recipe for mediocrity. The alternative is to set specific, difficult goals. Kurt Lewin, Edwin Locke and Gary Latham (Goal Setting Theory, in Organizational Behavior: Essential Theories of Motivation and Leadership, in John B.Miner, NY 2005), eminent organizational psychologists, have spent their careers studying the extraordinary effectiveness of setting specific and difficult goals. Difficult but possible is the key, "succeeding at something hard is more pleasurable, gives greater satisfaction and happiness, and increases your overall sense of well-being" (Grant Halverson, 2011). When you need to achieve a difficult, unfamiliar, complex goal, research shows that you should concentrate on the *how*, on the concrete nitty-gritty steps, on specific questions: what am I literally doing? On the other hand, when people think in 'why' terms, they are thinking about the bigger picture, what motivates them to achieve that goal. To get motivated, to enhance your self-control, research suggests thinking about 'why'. Another interesting aspect recent studies sustain is that our environment can trigger the unconscious pursuit of a goal. Studies have shown that the mere presence of means that could be used to achieve the goal can trigger it. I noticed that since I started leaving my books on the table without putting them away, it makes me work much harder every day, just like walking past the gym can trigger the goal of wanting to work out. If you pursue a goal or want others to pursue a goal, you can figure out ways to trigger your self-control and motivation or that of others. For example, the

The Name of the Game

kind of goal you end up choosing will determine not only how strong your motivation is, but also how long you will persist when the going gets tough. Understanding who succeeds and who gives up or fails in any achievement situation has been a major concern for scientific psychologists since the early 1940s. Most people assume it has a lot to do with intelligence and will-power, but that's surprisingly wrong. Grant Halvorson writes "how smart you are will influence the extent to which you experience something as difficult (for example how hard a math problem has to be before it stumps you), but it says *nothing* about how you will deal with difficulty when it happens. It says nothing about whether you will be persistent and determined or feel overwhelmed and helpless" (Grant Halvorson, 2011). That's why IQ tests don't supply all the answers about potential and future performance. Psychologists who study achievement have been particularly interested in the differences that arise when people focus on performing well to demonstrate ability (*being good*) versus focusing on progress, growth and gaining mastery (*getting better*). Psychologists refer to the desire to be good, i.e. to show that you are smart or talented or capable, or to outperform other people, as having a *performance goal*. Pursuing performance goals, energy is directed at achieving a particular outcome, we chose them because we think that reaching them will give us a sense of validation, ie. make us feel smart, talented, and desirable. In many studies we find that people pursuing performance goals are often the most productive and achieve higher results in given circumstances. But performance goals have a double-edged-sword quality – those ties to self-worth that make them so motivating are also what make them less adaptive

THE NAME OF THE GAME

when things become more complex and the going gets tougher. It's not just *people* that can be performance-goal oriented, you can also create a situation in which you make people slide into a performance goal environment. The nine-box grid is a good example of this kind of exercise. The nine-box grid gives a performance focus where people are plotted on a graph and compared to one another.

DILBERT © (2001) Scott Adams. Used By permission of UNIVERSAL UCLICK. All rights reserved

Companies very often make you slide into a performance goal environment. Of course it's not easy to find alternatives, but it's important to bear in mind what the consequences and side effects of this practice might be. When your goal is to get better, to develop or enhance your skills and abilities, psychologists call it a *mastery goal*. When pursuing mastery goals, people don't look for validation, they don't judge themselves worthy or unworthy, they judge themselves instead in terms of the *progress* they are making. It's about performance over time, it's about self-improvement, about becoming the best, most capable person you can be, rather than comparing yourself to others. Get-better goals can sometimes lead to the greatest achievements, because people rarely make the mistake of giving up too soon, setback is not a proof they aren't smart enough, it's just part of the journey. Studies have shown that the pursuit of be-good performance goals and get-better goals leads people to look, feel and behave very differently. We will focus on those differences because they are important to bear in mind when we assess talent and potential, since they can help us define what kind of potential we are looking for.

When I wrote that you can slide people into a fixed-mindset or a growth-mindset environment, or that you can slide them into a be-good or a get-better focus, I was referring to a series of studies Grant Halvorson and Laura Gelety ran in recent years with surprising results. They told participants that they were interested in problem solving. Half of the group was then told that their score on the problems they were about to work on reflected their "conceptual and analytical abilities" and that their goal should be to try to get a high score. In other words they were given a BE-GOOD goal. The other half of the group were told instead that the task was a "training tool", which would help them develop their abilities and they should "take advantage of this valuable learning opportunity". In other words they were given a GET-BETTER goal. The get better goal participants in the easier and more challenging conditions did equally well. But a very different picture emerged when it came to be-good performance goal pursuit, when difficulty or obstacles were introduced. The be-good group managed to solve significantly fewer problems. So, when the task gets difficult, and persistence is the key to higher achievement, get-better or mastery goals have a clear advantage. People might have the same goal, but a different focus. Psychologist Tory Higgins calls this focus either a promotion focused goal or a prevention focused goal. *Promotion focused* goals are thought about in terms of achievement and accomplishment. They are about having a focus on "*what will I gain from it?*" On the other hand, *prevention focused* goals are thought about in terms of safety and danger. They are about fulfilling responsibilities "*doing what you ought to do*", they are about "*minimizing losses*". Depending on whether you have a be-good approach or a get-better approach, a promotion or a prevention goal, you will make different choices, decide on different strategies and act differently. Higgins argues that the kind of goals we are pursuing reflect some of our basic needs. Two of our basic needs are to be loved and to be kept safe. In other words, we pursue *promotion goals* – seeking achievement and accomplishments – in order to be loved. Similarly, we pursue *prevention goals* - do what we ought to – to minimize losses and feel safe. When people have promotion goals, they feel free to be more exploratory and abstract in their thinking. They brainstorm and are particularly good at picking up on themes or synthetizing information. On the contrary, if you want to stay out of danger, you need to take action. Prevention focused thinking is concrete, it means choosing a plan sticking to it. You attend to specifics and stay out of trouble. Consequently, people who are prevention-minded are great with details. Why does it matter if we have one focus or the other, if we see our goals as achievements or as obligations? The difference between promotion-mindedness and prevention-mindedness has been shown to be enormously important in almost every aspect of our lives- it impacts the decisions we make, the strategies we use, our responses to setbacks and our very sense of well-being. Even though we all sometimes pursue both types of goals, it's also true that most of us come to have a dominant focus – we tend to think more about 'seeking achievement and accomplishment in order to be loved' (promotion focus) than about staying safe; or care more about being safe than about being loved (fulfilling responsibilities and avoiding mistakes, having thus a prevention focus: better safe than sorry). Higgins and his colleagues (E.T. Higgins et al, 2009) have shown that when we match our strategies to our goals, once we are conscious of these strategies, using the ones that 'feel right', we are more engaged, involved and persistent. We can manipulate goal focus. Galinsky (A.D.Galinsky and T.Mussweiler, 2001, pp.657-69) in one of his experiments observed how focus had a relevant impact on negotiation behavior and negotiation outcome. He made an experiment in which two groups of buyers had to negotiate the price of a plant; one group was given a promotion focus, while the second group a prevention focus. In the end, promotion-focused buyers purchased the plant for an average of nearly 4 million US$ less than prevention-minded buyers. The only difference was that one was thinking about what he had to gain, while the other was thinking about what he had to lose. Armed with an understanding of promotion and prevention-focus, so much of what we do (and what our friends, employees and bosses do) makes much more sense. Implicit theories are relevant when it comes to defining better strategies to reach our goals, however we can find these effects everywhere, especially in large organizations. When it comes to recruitment, assessing talent, or evaluating potential these theories should be kept in mind, because they have implications for people's choices and actions. They are implicit and define the name of the game. Depending upon the needs and values of the company, a 'be-good focus' in a given business model within a given economic context can be much more appropriate than a 'get-better' focus, or vice-versa. What do we want to value as an organization?

Chapter 2

THE NINE BOX GRID AND ITS IMPLICATIONS

PERFORMANCE VERSUS POTENTIAL: A LOGIC FALLACY

Falling into two major logic fallacies has become almost common practice when discussing potential. The first inductive fallacy refers to a number of articles and common IHRM practices where we find that potential is inferred from past performance. From general high-performance we cannot infer high-potential traits or indicators. We can make a bet. An example of inductive reasoning: all the swans we have seen are white, therefore all swans are white. Inductive reasoning or inductive logic is a kind of reasoning that constructs or evaluates propositions that are abstractions of observations of individual instances or members of the same class. It is commonly construed as a form of reasoning that makes generalizations based on individual instances. You might have seen some high-performers that made it up to general management positions, but that does not mean that all high-performers have CEO potential. This leads us to the second fallacy in the sense that high-potential criteria or traits cannot be inferred by analyzing

The Name of the Game

anecdotal success stories of people that highly performed, as CEOs might have by making it to the top. What brought about the success of one person in a given set of circumstances might bring about the downfall of another in a different context. In a few publications we find anecdotes told by some senior executives that made it to a CEO position where they list the key-criteria that determine the high-potential DNA, besides of course hard-work. The success of one does not give "legitimacy" to a theory, even if it might give some interesting insights. This inference, this inductive reasoning that takes into account personal experiences cannot imply a general rule. From various contingent situations that focus on performance most of the time, we cannot logically induce a general rule on high potential selection criteria. This reasoning, even if obvious for most of you, is intended to underline the fact that success and high performance in a given situation does not automatically imply potential and success in another. We often see books with titles like *The eleventh secret of the world's most successful executives* crowding the shelves of bookstores. These books might give some useful tips. But they are usually a list of unconnected pointers like "believe in yourself" or "be self-aware" or "take more risks!". As Carole S. Dweck writes "while you're left admiring people who can do that, it's never clear how these things fit together" and how much of the success depends on the context and the environment and many other variables that are not taken into account. So, you are inspired for a few days, but basically the world's most successful people still keep their secrets, the ten you forgot about and the eleventh you have a hard time grasping. The article by Groysberg and al. (HBR, may 2004) we discussed earlier in this paper, *The risky business of hiring stars,* showed how much the environment, the context, the organization's resources and capabilities, its internal systems and processes, the leadership's support and strong internal networks, not to mention trainings and mentoring - contributed to the success of a star. That's what Dweck means when she says that "you're left admiring people who can do that, but it's never clear how these things fit together", it is because the authors make abstractions of so many variables that contributed to the success, of so many aspects, that you never really get the whole picture. Over-simplification and generalization is a risky business.

Performance and potential are two distinct and independent variables, unless we prove they are linked using statistics. Silzer and Church (2009) have summarized and discussed the current state of literature and practice on potential and refer to this problem as "performance-potential paradox": a practice we know to be in some way inconsistent, but "paradoxically" we continue applying it. Silzer and Church say that performance and potential should not be linked too closely, however they assume that they cannot be treated as two independent variables. In my point of view this means admitting a paradox, but maintaining the logic fallacy. Saying performance and potential are linked in some way, without defining how and without being able to cite statistical data, means to fall back into the logic fallacy. The link between performance and potential remains an assumption that hasn't been proven yet. We can consider performance as a key variable to identify potential, because of its pragmatic use. Performance is a useful way to focus on those that already "do the job", leaving out those that are not up to expectations. Nevertheless, we cannot avoid thinking about the option where we might leave behind someone with great potential that underperformed for some reason, given that the number of variables that can determine performance are almost infinite. You will hardly unleash somebody's full potential if you set him in a fixed-mindset environment, giving him a be-good as well as a prevention focus. A person can be a high-performer in his current position but might have reached his limits in terms of competencies, skills, motivation or cognitive capabilities. Recent studies have shown that stress that derives from having to deal daily with a bad boss, can severely interfere with and undermine one's cognitive capabilities (Fiedler,F.E. 2001). This being said, I don't mean that performance assessment is not key for running businesses and identifying key-talent.

Silzer and Church described a well-known tool in which potential is plotted against performance: the nine box. In talent discussion – where the nine box is typically the tool that is used – potential is plotted against performance, resulting in a matrix of slots where employees are partitioned out. In practice, however, the borders are actually quite blurred. The nine-box is a useful tool, as it requires leaders to differentiate the capabilities between employees. The result is a separation of so-called "A" players from "B" players and "C" players. "A" being top performers with high-potential, according to this matrix. However, one of the fundamental problems with the traditional nine-box is that it links performance to potential without saying how and why they are linked. For the x-axis, we have measurement tools to assess different aspects impacting performance. However, for the y-axis, the potential axis remains much more a matter of "gut feeling". C. Robinson and al. (2009) state that potential and performance are two dependent variables, however they don't go further into the issue explaining the why and how of this dependence. They suggest that despite this problem the nine-box shouldn't be abandoned, but it's use should be revised, given the problems it continues to perpetuate.

To better understand this problem we have to go back to 1973. A significant part of the competence research base we rely on stems from a then-radical proposal by the late Harvard professor David McClelland (American Psychologist 28, 1973) titled "Testing for competence rather than intelligence". Interesting enough as we will see further on, when McClelland published this paper Richard Boyatzis and Daniel Golemann were his graduate students in psychology at Harvard. McClelland proposed that if an organization wanted to hire or promote the best person for a job, such as a leadership position, it should discard what were then the standard criteria. Instead of testing people for their IQ, technical skills, or personality – or just looking at their resumé - McClelland proposed first studying employees who were already outstanding performers in that job and systematically comparing them with those who were just average at it (Goleman, Boyatzis, McKee , *Primal Leadership*, 2002). That analysis yields not just the threshold abilities for the position (the basic skills everyone must have to do the job) but, more important, the *distinguishing* competencies: abilities that the

The Name of the Game

stars exhibited and the average performers did not. We don't have to forget that we are speaking of the best person for the job, meaning we are speaking of a well-defined position and competencies needed to cope with the responsibilities required for that given position. McClelland wasn't proposing a competency model to be applied in general to identify potential, he was just trying to minimize risks looking for past performance, identifying the top performers in that role or a similar role in a given context. We have the impression that the reflex of looking only at top performers became over time a useful "shortcut" towards identifying stars. This does not mean that it's the only possible way to identify top talent.

Lyle Spencer, a longtime associate of McClelland, developed a competences model for an industrial firm where he identified the top performers. The stars were compared with managers whose performance was only average and the two groups underwent intensive interviews designed to assess competencies. Four competencies that also derive from *emotional intelligence* emerged as the unique strength of the stars compared to the average performers: the *drive* to achieve results, the ability to take *initiative*, skills in *collaboration* and networking and the *ability to lead* teams. This was true for this industrial company at that time within a given context. Almost 40 years later, further traits were added to those 4 "strengths" or "qualities", just to name a few: agile learning abilities, cognitive flexibility, adaptability, self-awareness. Most companies and consulting firms don't refer to the same ones and have different 'high-potential models' in which the crucial qualities differ. Definitions are also rarely given, so that those qualities and traits remain some sort of quest for a mystical grail. In this paper we will discuss key themes across current models of potential. The aim is to try and cast some light on what differentiate these models and in particular to see what lies behind the terms (e.g. what do we refer to when we speak of learning agility? Or when we speak of cognitive adaptability or flexibility?). Those definitions are key to a better understanding of this topic.

C. Robinson and al. (2009) affirms that current job performance is best thought of as a necessary but insufficient indicator of potential. They propose an alternative to the nine-box that accounts for the interdependency of both variables. In terms of logic consistency we don't agree with the interdependency of the two variables, however the exercise of looking at their alternative model might be useful if we assume that it's a pragmatic way and a kind of "shortcut" to have rapid access and visibility of the "high performing" talent pool. What sets their model apart from the nine-box is that it helps leaders make decisions based on a number of steps that go beyond job performance. Those steps should guide more robust and constructive discussions about promotional decision making. They call this model the *potential pyramid*, which is a process that presents an ascending hierarchy of decision steps or checkpoints. If the person meets or exceeds expectations at one step, he/she is then considered against the next.

The Name of the Game

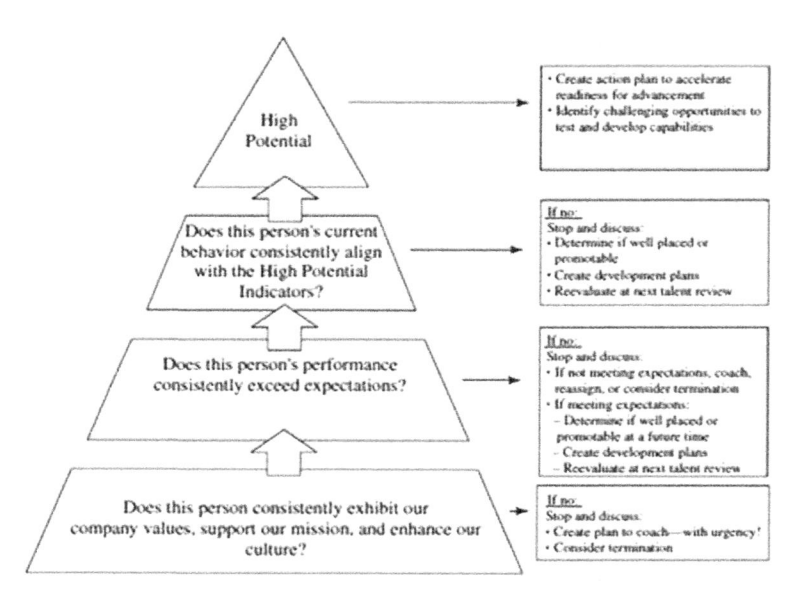

```
                    /\
                   /  \
                  / High\          → • Create action plan to accelerate
                 /Potential\          readiness for advancement
                /_____\      • Identify challenging opportunities to
                     ⇧              test and develop capabilities
         /Does this person's current\     If no:
        / behavior consistently align \   Stop and discuss:
       /   with the High Potential     \ → • Determine if well placed or
      /         Indicators?             \   promotable
     /_____\ • Create development plans
                     ⇧                    • Reevaluate at next talent review
       /Does this person's performance\    If no:
      /  consistently exceed expectations?\  Stop and discuss:
     /                                     \→ • If not meeting expectations, coach,
    /                                       \   reassign, or consider termination
   /_____\ • If meeting expectations:
                     ⇧                          - Determine if well placed or
                                                  promotable at a future time
    /Does this person consistently exhibit our\    - Create development plans
   / company values, support our mission, and  \   - Reevaluate at next talent review
  /          enhance our culture?               \  If no:
 /_____\ Stop and discuss:
                                                  → • Create plan to coach—with urgency!
                                                    • Consider termination
```

Figure 1. Potential pyramid.

(C.Robinson et al., 2009, p. 414)

At the third level we find the question: does this person's current behavior consistently align with the High-potential indicators? The authors give some hints of what those high potential indicators might include, such as mental agility, natural curiosity, self-development and resilience in the face of adversity, but nothing is defined and the reader does not understand what it implies. What I would retain is the term indicator rather than criteria. Criteria better applies to assessing past actions, while an indicator is a not-yet validated future accomplishment. An interesting point that emerges in the article is that if an employee does not embody what the company stands for in terms of values, then all the "potential" in the world may not prove worthy of becoming reality and be released. Thus, a high-potential in a company that highly values initiative and entrepreneurship might never succeed in a different organization with different values. Using this model is a bit like looking into a pool of "usual suspects" that have been on the fast-track for years, probably overlooking many high potential employees that don't fit exactly into the mold. Introducing at this point the theory of non-linear dynamics might give us some insight into these issues.

NON-LINEAR DYNAMICS

Mark E. Mendenhall and al. published an article in the Human Resource Management review titled *Non-linear Dynamics: a new perspective on IHRM research and practice in the 21st Century* (1998). This article introduces the reader to one of the paradigms that is emerging as a threat to logical positivism's reign as the dominant paradigm in the field of management: non-linear dynamics. Social scientists have traditionally operated from the assumption that human systems are being composed of relationships among variables that exist and operate according to linear, cause-effect laws (Mendenhall and Macomber 1997). Thus the goal for most social scientists is to isolate cause-effect relationships within organizational systems; they operate from the belief that one can "break a linear system up into its components, study and explain each component, then put it all back together and…have the explanation of the whole" (Parker and Stacey 1994). Mathematics provides a very useful, powerful set of tools for working with such systems, as long as the equations, or their differentials, are linear. Non-linearity is difficult to conceptualize because most of us view the world

The Name of the Game

through linear perspectives and assumptions. Meiss (1995) defines non-linearity this way:

"In algebra we define linearity in terms of functions which have the property $f(x+y) = f(x)+f(y)$ and $f(ax) = af(x)$. Non-linear is defined as the negation of linear. This means that the result may be out of proportion to the input "x" or "y". Thus the fundamental simplifying tools of linear analysis are no longer available."

Linearity has definitely something reassuring, it gives the impression that we can master and control the input and outcome. In such non-linear systems, a cause does not have one and only one effect – the system is made up of *variables that mutually influence each other* in extremely complex ways, so that the distinction between independent and dependent variables, interaction effects, and causation become blurred. In non-linear systems, the relationship of the parts within the system are so mutually interwined that one cannot simply tear out a subsystem of a larger system and study it. It cannot be done because each element of the system is too richly interconnected with other elements of the system (Mendenhall, 1997, p. 45 N°41). Research studies have shown that many non-linear dynamical systems are highly sensitive to small deviations. That is, a small difference at the beginning of a series of values or at some intervals soon magnifies into major differences among evolving systems. The explanation of the importance of small factors comes through the circumstance that *non-linear dynamical systems depend on feedback.* As opposed to Newtonian concepts, which more clearly differentiate between causes and effects, feedback is the notion that an effect becomes part of the cause in subsequent iterations of the system's internal operations (Lichtenstein et al, 1997, Mendenhall and Macomber 1997). Prediction beyond a very limited time period therefore becomes impossible, although general patterns are discernible, "deep ordering principles" or "attractors" that embody the long-term qualitative behavior of the system (Capra, 1996). The component parts of a non-linear system have been named "adaptive agents" being in their nature active rather than passive. Whether an adaptive agent is a single-cell organism, a manager, a high-potential or a nation's economy, they are changing strategy in order to adapt to on-going change. Thus, by looking through non-linear dynamic lenses or spectacles, we should ask to what degree the model represents the actual dynamics of the phenomenon it contends to model. We would say that too few arrows connect too few variables, and that the arrows should have heads on both ends, reflecting the mutual influence between variables, shouldn't they? The linear model might be rationally elegant, simplifying things and providing some clarity on a phenomenon, but to what degree does the clarification fit with the reality of the adjustment process? If we think again of the article by Groysberg and al. *The risky business of hiring stars* (HBR 2004), even if structured according to cause-effect logic, it gave us some insights on the inter-dependence of variables that presupposed a non-linear dynamics approach.

The holy grail of being able to predict human behavior does not exist within the paradigm of non-linear systems (Bak and Chen 1991, Capra 1996, Mendenhall and Macomber 1997). Mendanhall proposes, what seems to me a sound paradigmatic shift, from a linear to non-linear paradigm which implies the

The Name of the Game

need to have the goal of *understanding* rather than *predicting*, once we approach human social phenomena. Currently however, what we do as HR managers or HR consultants is to continually attempt to superimpose linear plans, processes, and models onto existing organizational processes that are non-linear. When we superimpose linearity onto non-linear reality, we create policies and practices that are incongruent with the context in which they exist. This leads to unintended dysfunctional HR consequences, such as expecting that a newly hired star through executive search will continue being a star in a new company because that is part of the strategic program and plan.

Scott Adams has become a multimillionaire by parodying this state of affairs: Dilbert exists because we continually try to understand non-linear systems from linear mindsets, and act in non-linear organizational systems according to linear mindsets:

DILBERT © (2007) Scott Adams. Used By permission of UNIVERSAL UCLICK. All rights reserved

In a recent article by C. Fenandez-Araoz, B.Groysbeg and N. Nohria (Harvard Business Review October 2011) potential was defined as follows: potential indicates whether someone will be able to succeed in a bigger role in the future. It's a person's ability to grow and to handle responsibilities of greater scale and scope. By "greater scales" we mean a job in the same area but with, say, a larger budget or staff; by greater scope we mean a job involving activities of substantially more breadth and complexity. Interviewing senior HR leaders, depending upon the organization's processes, the high-potential label meant readiness to go up two (hierarchical) levels in a period of 3-5 years in some cases, in other organizations two upward moves in up to 3 years. One of the organizations called high-potentials "best bets", those ready to move up to executive roles. The fact of acknowledging reality, acknowledging the fact that you aren't reading a crystal ball, but that according to a given set of performance data and variables you are doing what appears to be a "best bet", appeared to be a sound approach.

The fast-track career approach is based on the assumption that people learn from experience. G. Graen (2009) denounces a focus on potential as harmful, instead of speaking of potential in general terms he prefers speaking of "readiness". Readiness is evaluated via functional assessment and it might determine the speed of promotion towards a *target-job*. He does not speak explicitly of potential, but of useful predictors or indicators of long-term career success: cognitive skills, interpersonal skills, adaptability, learning and leadership skills, and of course motivation. Besides the fact that they "sound good", once again it's not clear what lies behind those terms. Is it learning agility he is referring to or a "general" panel of leadership skills?

The Name of the Game

Two other studies one by P.G. Dominick and A.S. Gabriel (2009) titled *Two sides to the story: an interactionist perspective on identifying potential*, the other by P.A. Heslin (2009) *"Potential in the eye of the beholder: the role of managers who spot rising stars"*, underline the importance of an additional variable : <u>who</u> is assessing potential and how. Is it the manager whom the employee reports to? Is it the Business Unit director, two levels above? Is it both of them including the HRs? Are they trained to carry out assessments? Is their assessment based on competencies and skills assessment? Does it include personality assessment? Dominick and Gabriel refer to another variable or "adaptive agent" of a non-linear system. They see a facet of the non-linear system when they speak of *interactionist perspective*. Competencies assessment should be learned and it should not be a single person's perspective and perception that should validate "high potential labeling". Furthermore, this assessment has an impact on the person being assessed, depending on <u>what</u> is said and <u>how</u> it is said. The 'what' and the 'how' might have a very big impact on the person who has been assessed and if we think according to the "interactionist model" also a big impact on the organization, not merely in the short term, but in the long term as we will see later on when analyzing the data we derived from the interviews. Dominick and Gabriel encourage a broader perspective on identification and propose a fluid and dynamic construct that is based on social system factors as well as on individual differences in skills and capabilities, implying the importance of an organization development philosophy that encourages human growth, learning and development. Thus focusing on the interaction between the assessor and the assessed and always working on a growth and development assumption across all levels of employees.

What should be now considered is identifying specific competencies and traits that are necessary to become an effective talent assessor. That's why in my personal opinion talent review meetings and calibration sessions are so important, since the perception of many is unlikely to be completely biased by personal judgments. Dominick and Gabriel (2009) make the point that self-awareness in managers might reduce their perceptual biases. However we might say that self-awareness is useful for any kind of judgment, being it a meta-cognitive exercise. Meta-cognitive exercise helps to avoid biases due to personal perceptions, which are dependent on education, values, references, culture and many other factors.

Yost and Chang (2009) have a similar view of development but a different view of potential. They introduce their idea of potential as place and process. They suggest that by using these two dimensions you can essentially develop potential against a host of possible roles and job configurations in an organization. They believe organizations should not focus on creating the 'haves' and the 'have nots', but a more fluid developmentally focused workplace. Church and Silzer agree partially with this position, but they state that from a pragmatic perspective organizations do need some method of differentiating talent in order to make selection, promotions and take decisions. In their opinion Yost and Chang's point of view is somewhat unrealistic or idealistic. What I personally would retain of Yost and Chang position is quite different from Silzer and Church's point of view. Yost and Chang don't mean that evaluation is unnecessary, but rather than ticking the boxes of what one has or hasn't, we need to see how to develop each and every one. It doesn't mean that everybody can make it to the top, not least also because not everyone wishes to become a CEO, but rather think in terms of places and process, considering available positions and the person's competencies and what options there are for development and learning.

The nine-box model requires sustained effort to separate these two dimensions conceptually. Being one dimension more a bet than a dimension. Mone and al. (2009) suggest that practitioners take a multi-year view of performance (vs. focusing just on the current year) to help eliminate this confusion. Silzer and Church propose using a 3-year performance history, but a high-potential won't spend most of the time three years in the same position before the organization starts considering whether to promote him. A Senior Human Resources Director working for one of the major financial institutions we interviewed said that they had introduced two non-consecutive years of high-performance over a period of three years as a rule to validate high-potential.

Most of the time there is however little agreement within and between organizations on the definitions and components of the concept of potential. Church and Silzer in another recent article titled *The pearls and Perils of Identifying Potential* (Industrial and Organizational Psychology 2, 2009, pp.377-412) introduce a new integrated model of potential that incorporates previous literature and current assessment practice regarding high-potentials. It provides a useful and coherent structure of potential, and is reflective of a variety of different talent pools. The key question that many articles do not consider is: *potential, what for?* Interviewing two senior Head of Executive Talent executives we found out that besides a high-potential talent pool where management and leadership skills were the focus, they recently started to create a second high-potential talent pool called the "experts" high-potential talent pool. When we think of potential, we should therefore always be specific and not generic. What is this potential for? Silzer and Church's model proposes a three dimensional integrated model that includes: a) foundational dimension; b) growth dimension; c) career dimensions. This model will be discussed in more detail in the following chapter.

What concerns about this approach is that at the very center of talent management there is a practice area called "high-potential talent" that has already become in some cases, or will become, a field of its own. Two superimposed structures, one to manage talent in general, the lower caste, and another dedicated to high potentials, the labeled stars, the upper caste. The problem is when special begins to mean better than others: a more valuable human being, a superior person, an entitled person. Organizations need team work. If they create a fixed-mindset environment and a culture of castes, of superstars, then they should start measuring the consequences. We saw the perils of this kind of approach and explained the limits, not only from an organizational perspective, but also from a motivational one.

THE TALENT WAR AND ITS IMPLICATIONS

The turning point in some way has been an article published in 1997 by McKinsey that introduced the theme "war for talent" that on one hand expressed a concern and the idea that identifying and managing high-potential talent has become increasingly important for organizations, giving rise to a new tendency, and on the other hand contributed to what can be described as an obsession. This was the first of many other articles on this theme. The 'war for talent' created some kind of urgency on this topic that in my point of view gave way to some positive and some far from positive, talent management practices and policies. Silzer and Church report that one hundred percent of 20 major corporations surveyed in 2008 have a high-potential program. However there are major differences between organizations concerning those "potential programs". Radical potential program differences mean that those organizations have different cultures, value different things and have sometimes opposed or very different mindsets. High-potential programs represent in a sense a shortcut enabling anyone to have a rapid insight into the culture and values of an organization, they give access to the instructions of the 'game'.

Silzer and Dowell propose that talent management "is an integrated set of processes, programs and cultural norms in an organization designed and implemented to attract, develop, deploy, and retain talent to achieve strategic objectives and meet future business needs". Sometimes however those integrated processes and programs employ practices that are thought to attract and retain talent and increase motivation, but may prove shortsighted since they are short-term approaches. They don't consider some interesting breakthroughs made in cognitive-, developmental-, social- and personality-clinical psychology that have focused, for example, on how people cope with failure as we saw in Dweck's Mindset theory. People may start with different temperaments and different aptitudes, but it is clear that experience, training and personal effort take them the rest of the way. The growth mindset is based on the belief that your basic qualities can be cultivated through your efforts. Although people may differ in every way – in their initial talents and aptitudes, interests, or temperaments – everyone can grow through application and experience. The passion, the will and ambition to stretch yourself and stick to something, even (and especially) if it's not going well, is the hallmark of the growth mindset (Dweck, 2006). For the fixed mindset, risk and effort are two things that might reveal your inadequacies and show that you were not up to the task. In fact, it is startling to see the degree to which people with fixed-mindset do not believe in effort. What Dweck's research showed isn't just that people happen to recognize the value of challenging themselves and the importance of effort. Her research has shown that this *comes directly* from the growth-mindset, *with its focus on development and learning, these ideas about challenge and effort follow*. What was even more fascinating in reading Dweck's research is the possibility of putting people (temporarily) in a fixed mindset. Joseph Martocchio conducted a study of employees who were

The Name of the Game

taking a short computer training course. Half the employees were put in a fixed mindset. He told them it was all about how much natural ability they had. The other half were put in a developmental mindset. He told them that computer skills could be developed. Although the two groups started with exactly the same skill level, by the end of the training things looked very different. Those put into a growth mindset, despite their many errors were confident about their capabilities. Those put in a fixed mindset lost confidence as they learned. With its focus on permanent traits, people quickly fear challenge and devalue effort. The fact of putting people into a fixed-mindset had quite negative consequences. If for example we decide to label top talent and formally communicate who's on the high-potential list, we are proceeding in a way that implies giving highly talented employees a mark of gratitude, a sign of recognition they may feel proud of. All will be well as long as those happy few face only successes; in case of setbacks we saw that generic-praise might be a slippery path. A recent paper published by the Center for Creative leadership by Michael Campbell and Roland Smith titled *High-Potential Talent – A view from inside the Leadership Pipeline* examines talent management through the eyes of high-potential managers. They surveyed 199 leaders attending CLL's development programs. The findings have implications for how organizations identify, invest in, and leverage their high-potential talent. They assert that 77 percent of them "place a high degree of importance on being formally identified as a high-potential" in their organization. They found that high-potentials "feel good about their status, the reason why being formally recognized as high-potentials is considered important". The fact high-potentials used the term 'status', means that they shifted into a fixed-mindset. If they experience a setback, it means that their self-worth is at stake. Status means validation. In this study, however, the authors write that a number of high-potentials (percentage not communicated) reported that there is a downside to this status, like for example a feeling of increasing pressure and anxiety around high expectations or performance. In my view this study gives interesting insights. The paper associates the importance of telling high-potentials formally they have been identified and selected, with the need of high-potentials to have a clear career path. These factors are not interdependent. The fact of knowing they have been identified should imply higher commitment and engagement. The point I would make is that you don't need to label people and tell them formally that they are high-potentials in order to help them identify a career path. They don't need to know they are high-potentials in order to feel engaged and committed. If you need to reassure them about their status, you should start having some doubts about their actual potential. I agree that it might appear as a strong sign of recognition; however are we really doing those future organizational leaders a favor by labeling them and telling them they are hypo? Over half of the participants in this study indicated that their organization has a formal process for identifying high-potential employees. It's one thing to imply from various signals you receive – such as being invited to join a leadership program – that you may be on the list and identified as high-potential, it's another thing to be informed formally as if it were a generic trait you were born with. Still another to be informed that you have been identified as high-potential, but that it's a judgment given in a particular context and at a given moment and it might change over time. M.Campell and A.Smith's study is about telling or not telling, it's either black or white. It misses the interesting aspects of all the shades of grey that are key to having a better understanding of this subject. It's not about yes or no, it's about when, what and how. The authors of this study want to make a point by saying that 91 percent of participants in the leadership program are informed about their status, stating that official recognition, it seems, fosters the leader's identity as a high-potential. Are we sure we want to create and foster leaders with a high-potential identity? Referring to high-potential identity means referring to a stable and unchanging trait. This means creating a fixed mindset environment in which employees will adapt to the rules of the game. As we saw in Dweck's article about generic and non-generic praise, subtle linguistic cues affect motivation. If there is something organizations should care about, it is their key talent's motivation. More important than having a high-potential identity is having self-insight and being able to have accurate views about one's assets and limitations. Studies show that people can be terrible at estimating their own abilities. Another of Dweck's studies showed that it was those with the fixed mindset who accounted for almost all the inaccuracy. The people with growth mindset were amazingly accurate when doing self-assessment. Thinking about it, it makes sense. If, like those with the growth mindset, you believe you can develop yourself, then you are open to accurate information about your current abilities, even if it's sometimes unflattering.

THE NINE BOX GRID AND ITS IMPLICATIONS

What's more, if you are oriented towards learning and development, you need accurate information about current abilities in order to learn effectively. However, if everything is either good or bad news about your precious stable status and traits – as it is with fixed mindset people – distortions inevitably enter the picture. Some outcomes are magnified, others justified by external causes and explained away, and before you know it you don't manage to have a clear insight about yourself. Howard Gardner, in his book *Extraordinary Minds* concluded that exceptional individuals have "*a special talent for identifying their own strengths and weaknesses*". Dweck concludes that it's interesting to note that her researches show that those with the growth mindset seem to have that talent. The passion for stretching yourself and sticking to it, even – or especially- when it's not going well, is the hallmark of the growth mindset, people who are able to acknowledge their weaknesses and strive to do better. Convert life's setbacks to into future success. In one case, failure is about having a setback. Getting a bad grade, failing an important project, getting rejected. It means you're not smart or talented. In the other case, failure is about not growing. Not reaching for the things you value, having the feeling you're not fulfilling your potential. In this second scenario you need to know your strengths and weaknesses, work on them in order to grow. In the other one effort is a bad thing and failure means you are not smart enough. If you were, you wouldn't need effort. You can see the difference in mindsets in the lab, watching brain waves in an IRM experiment. Dweck tested brain waves at Columbia's lab. As the growth mindset group answered difficult questions and got feed-back,

The Name of the Game

they noticed when observing the brain waves that they showed utmost attention and interest. People with fixed-mindset were only showing interest and attention when the feedback reflected on their ability. Their brain waves were recording high levels of attention to the answer right or wrong, but as soon as they received negative feedback and were presented with information that could help them learn from the mistake, there was no sign of interest anymore, no waves on the screen. Even when they had got an answer wrong, they were not interested in learning what the right answer was. NASA found an interesting way to judge potential. When they were soliciting applications for astronauts, they rejected people with pure histories of success and instead selected people who had had a significant failure and bounced back from it. Even in growth mindset, failure can be a painful experience. But it does not define you. It's a situation, a problem that must be faced, dealt with and learned from. Isn't potential someone's capacity to learn and develop their skills over time? Or do you think that it's a natural gift a person possesses and he needs to prove it over and over again?

In one study they showed how students responded to an academic failure – a poor test grade in one course. Those with the growth-mindset, said they would study harder for the next test. But those with the fixed mindset said they would study less for the next test. If they don't have the ability, why waste time? Some even seriously considered cheating! Cheating and lying is another issue correlated with fixed mindset. In other experiments Dweck recorded that almost 40 percent of those who had a fixed mindset when asked to disclose their negative scores in a test preferred lying about their results instead of telling the truth. Believing that success is about learning, students with the growth mindset don't look for excuses when they fail. But those with the fixed mindset don't want to expose their deficiencies and prefer lying or look for excuses. Believing talent can be developed allows people to fulfill their potential. The growth mindset does allow people to love what they're doing – and continue loving it in face of hardship, difficulties and setback. Success for growth mindset is a by-product of their passion and enthusiasm for what they are doing. In the fixed mindset, everything is about the outcome. What about workaholics having a fixed mindset? Those people may be free of the a priori belief that high effort equals low ability, but they have the other aspects of the fixed mindset, as we will see further on when discussing the "CEO disease".

If fixed mindset facing setbacks presents certain risks, fixed-mindset people in a fixed-mindset environment present exponentially higher risks. Fostering leaders with a high potential identity means encouraging this exponential risk to occur. People who believe in fixed traits feel an urgency to succeed as we already mentioned, and when they do, they may feel more than pride. They may feel a sense of superiority, since success means that their fixed traits are better than other people's.

Furthermore, if they work in a fixed-mindset environment their appreciations and perceptions will be confirmed, they will have the organization's legitimacy to feel better than others. Fostering leaders high-potential identity means incurring in

The Name of the Game

this kind of scenario : people who will develop an entitled sense of superiority.

The good news is that if you are in a fixed mindset you can change your mindset into a growth mindset. If you are a Head of Global Talent you can make sure your practices and policies are growth mindset oriented, contributing to a developmental environment where learning, effort and personal and organizational development are key. Studies by Pete Heslin, Don VandeWalle and Gary Latham showed that many executives do not believe in personal change. These fixed-mindset managers just look for *existing* talent and performance, they judge their employees as competent or incompetent from the outset and that's it. In France sometimes they just judge from the "grande école" label on the resume. They provide relatively little developmental training or coaching and remain stuck in their initial impression. What's more, they are far less likely to seek or accept critical feedback from their employees. We have talked about all the well-meaning parents and teachers who have tried to boost their children's self-esteem by telling them how smart and talented they are. And we have talked about all the negative effects of this kind of praise.

Well, those children have now entered the workforce and have invented the war for talent. And sure enough they can't function unless they are getting a sticker or a medal for every move. We now have a workforce full of people who need constant reassurance and can't take criticism; they avoid feedback and are partisans of "*groupthinking*". This isn't a good recipe for success in business, where taking on challenges, showing resilience and persistence and most of all, admitting and correcting mistakes are essential. In the past ten years we have various examples of arrogance, of fixed-mindset managers working in a fixed mindset environment. Does Enron or the 'Kerviel affaire' within Sociéte Générale ring a bell? How did Enron, such a spectacular promise turn in to such a devastating disaster? It was incompetence, it was corruption, but according to Malcolm Gladwell writing in The New Yorker, it may have been also mindset. American corporations became obsessed with talent. McKinsey insists, as do many other consulting firms, that "talent mindset" is key to success. Just as there are "naturals" in sports, there are "naturals" in business. As Gladwell writes, "This 'talent mindset' is the new orthodoxy of American management". Enron recruited stars and put absolute faith in talent. But by doing so Enron did a fatal thing: it created a culture that worshipped talent, therefore putting their employees in a fixed mindset environment, forcing them to look and act extraordinarily talented. People with fixed mindset don't admit failure and don't correct deficiencies. They keep going until it's too late. A company that cannot self-correct cannot thrive. Highly talented people who cannot assess their deficiencies and lack a critical attitude won't become great leaders.

I mentioned the term groupthink above. In the early 1970s, Irving Janis coined the term 'groupthink'. It's when everyone in a group starts thinking alike. No one has a different opinion, no one dares to express a divergent view. No one disagrees. It can lead to catastrophic decisions, and as the Wood Study suggests (Robert Wood and Albert Bandura), it often derives

The Name of the Game

from a fixed mindset. In their study, they created fixed-mindset and growth-mindset managers, by making them slip into a fixed-mindset or growth-mindset environment where they had to run a simulated organization. Half the group was given a fixed-mindset, the other half a growth mindset. They were told that the task measured their basic, underlying abilities in the fixed-mindset. Thus, the higher the capacity, the better they would perform. The other group were told that management skills were developed through practice and that the task would give them an opportunity to cultivate their skills. The fixed-mindset did not really profit from their mistakes, the task was demanding and they were worried about measuring each other's capabilities and tended towards consensus. They were afraid to expose themselves and show their deficiencies and tended to "groupthink", which is reassuring in a fixed mindset environment. But those with the growth mindset kept learning, they looked directly at their mistakes, used the feedback and altered their strategies exposing their views in an open discussion. Groupthink can occur when people put unlimited faith in a talented leader, a star. Charisma can be a danger in some way. Jim Collins in his book "*Good to Great*", which is the result of a five year study, tried to find out what distinguished the thriving company from others. He selected eleven companies whose stock returns had consistently increased relatively to other companies in the same industry, and who managed to maintain this edge for at least another 5 years. He found that there were several factors that contributed to this success, but the one that was absolutely key was the type of leader who in every case led the company into greatness. These were not "big egos" charismatic types that self-proclaimed their talent and how brilliant they were. They were self-effacing people who constantly asked questions, asked for feed-back and who were resilient enough to confront the most negative and worst news – that is the ability to face failures, even their own, while maintaining faith that they would succeed in the end. They stuck to the plan and corrected deficiencies. Winston Churchill set up a special department and the job of this department, Jim Collins reports, was to give Churchill the worst news, the negative feedback about recent operations and decisions. Then Churchill could sleep well, knowing he had not been "groupthinked" into a false sense of security. Groupthink can happen when the group gets carried away by success followed by a sense of brilliance and superiority, as we experienced recently with the toxic assets scandal. Groupthink can also happen when a fixed-mindset manager punishes dissent. People may not stop thinking critically, but they stop speaking up. There are many ways in which the fixed-mindset creates groupthink. Leaders are perceived as all-powerful, as gods that never err. Fixed mindset leaders conceive the world as a place where some people are superior and some are inferior. They feel the urgent need to affirm over and over again that they are superior, and the company or the State is simply a platform for this. If I was to give an example, I would think of the past 15 years in Italy. Berlusconi used Italy as his personal platform. He was invulnerable, invincible, entitled to everything he could think of, always worried about what would make him feel and look good instead of what would serve longer-term goals. He blamed others, covering mistakes, crushed rivals, screwed the

The Name of the Game

little guy: these are the standard operating procedures be it in leading a corporation or in leading a country. Another point is that those great geniuses don't want to surround themselves with great teams either. Dweck noticed that fixed-mindset people want to be the only "big-fish", so that when they compare themselves to those around them they can feel above the rest. Collins in his book "*Good to Great*" notes that in many companies he studied the leader became the primary worry, the main thing people worried about. "The minute a leader allows himself to become the primary reality people worry about, rather than reality being the primary reality, you have a recipe for mediocrity, or worse". Before the leader allows himself to become the primary reality there are signs however that should not be overlooked. It's when you notice a growing gap between rhetoric and practice. By that I mean that the leader's discourse affirms one thing and the practice demonstrates another, most of the time the opposite. Do you think we will have a hard time finding leaders in the future? Why has succession planning become one of the most highly rewarded and key consultanting activities in the past ten years? If businesses don't play a role in developing a more mature and growth-minded workforce, more autonomous, critical and entrepreneurial talent pipeline, where will the leaders of the future come from? They won't come from Peter Cappelli's talent management model inspired from supply chain management either (P. Cappelli, *Talent on Demand*, 2008). He suggests estimating the cheapest and fastest ways of matching supply to anticipated demand, deciding what to outsource, what to give to temporary workers, and which talent to hire 'on demand', since developing talent means taking the risk of losing it to the competition. The idea is to minimize risk, develop as little as you can to avoid this risk and minimize costs. This means focusing on performance and competencies and not on potential. It means hiring people that tick competency boxes and won't be given a chance to develop, since the mode is a "plug and play" mode.

The challenge ahead isn't a war for talent, it's about switching to a more mature, growth-minded and long-term paradigm.

Before exploring the different talent and high-potential programs we identified by interviewing senior HR executives of fifteen international corporates, we will consider the different variables that are used to identify and assess performance and potential. The variables that corporations have chosen, are indicators of the corporate's culture and values. What is potential for? Are we valuing and supporting creative and innovative thinking, an autonomous and entrepreneurial approach? Or are we valuing performance? Are we supporting particular skills, abilities and technical knowledge in a given area, say asset management?

Chapter 3

COGNITIVE POTENTIAL: WHY WE WASTE TALENT

COGNITIVE POTENTIAL: CRYSTALLIZED-AND FLUID INTELLIGENCE

All potential models have cognitive abilities as one of the main factors, some conceive it as a foundational variable, meaning that it is mostly innate and difficult to change over time; while others conceive it as mostly developmental; most affirm that it is partly inborn and partly developmental. Depending upon the potential model (every consulting company has its own model as we will see in the next chapter) terms are employed in different contexts and mixed up in such a way that it is difficult to know what the terms are referring to. *Learning agility*, for example, is classified as a cognitive factor in some models, while in others it is a developmental aspect defined as learning capacity. In the well-known article by Michael Lombardo "High-Potentials as High-learners" (2002) intelligence is defined as a "characteristic that doesn't change much and can be detected early...potential, in our definition,

The Name of the Game

involves learning new skills, learning from experience, acumen or agility in order to perform in first-time situations". Two of the studies at the Center for Creative Leadership (McCall, Lombardo and Morrison, 1998) found that if people have certain powerful on-the-job experiences and learn from them, that is a sign of long-term success. Sternberg, Wagner, William and Horvath (1995) identify street-smarts (those that learn from experience) as far more correlated with the hierarchical level attained in organizations than IQ. In a similar vein, emotional intelligence (McClelland, Goleman 1998) has been related to performance. Nevertheless, the article does not explain the relation between learning agility, experience, IQ, emotional intelligence and performance. The reader gets lost, because often there is a problem of definition, the terms are employed indiscriminately (i.e. cognitive agility, learning agility, adaptability, dealing with complexity, strategic thinking…etc.) and it is difficult to understand which is the inborn trait, which the developmental part and how they are related to each other, if at all. Since the publication of these articles ten years ago, cognitive psychology experiments in neuroscience have come a long way. That's why I found it interesting to plunge into the latest theories about intelligence as a way to answer those questions.

Important progress has been made in the neurosciences in recent years thanks to magnetic resonance imaging (MRI). MRI gave access to the brain circuitry, which permitted an insight into different ability factors and how they relate.

HISTORICAL BACKGROUND

More than a century ago Jacobs (1887) invented memory span as a test of intellect, and since then psychologists have made important progress in measuring intellectual capabilities. Since Spearman's demonstration of the general ability factor (g), *general intelligence,* who first put intelligence testing in the framework of scientific research, the field has experienced major theoretical developments. Cattel and Horn (*Theory of Fluid and Crystallized intelligence a critical experiment, 1963, Cattel 1961 and Cattel and Horn 1967*) are the originators of the Fluid- and Crystallized (Gf and Gc) theory of intelligence:

*"The theory of 'fluid and crystallized general abilities', which states that with more refined analytical methods the general ability factor (g) now measured by intelligence tests will be found to be not one factor but **two**. In spite of marked cooperativeness of loading pattern, which makes them difficult to separate, they have properties differing in vital ways for educational and clinical prediction'. (R.B. Cattell, Journal of Educational Psychology, 1963, vol.54, N°1, p.1-22).*

The two factors Gf and Gc have different properties: Crystallized ability loads more highly those cognitive performances in which skilled judgment habits have become consolidated, as for example earlier learning application (verbal and numerical primaries, or achievement in geography or history). Fluid intelligence (Gf), on the other hand, shows more in tests requiring adaptation to new situations where crystallized skills are of no particular advantage[2]. Crystallized intelligence

---

[2] Thomas,David.C. et al.'s (2012) see the construct of cultural intelligence, which seems to be related in many ways to the fluid intelligence factor.

The Name of the Game

is related to experience and notions we learned in our lives, while fluid intelligence is related to the ability to adapt to new situations, complex problem solving and defining strategies. At the present time research on these theories is as vital in the applied as in the basic field, as is the case in human resources management. For if the main concepts are correct, affirmed Cattell over 50 years ago, present routine testing practices in school or at work (IQ), are wasting a lot of talent, since they tend to measure mostly crystallized intelligence, unless they use the Raven's matrices test. The traditional intelligence test, because it confounds fluid with crystallized intelligence and even with the third-order general attainment factor (g = general intelligence or ability), gives speciously non-specific correlations and results. Cattel[3] gives the example of tests in schools that are supposed to predict future achievement. A test in June predicts academic achievement in June, for the simple reason that it already surreptitiously contains in itself most of the criterion it is claiming to predict. Thus the importance of distinguishing the three factors Fluid Intelligence G(f), Crystallized Intelligence G(c) and General ability factor (g), understanding what are the abilities associated with every factor and how they are interrelated, if at all. In the writings of Lombardo and al. learning agility is described as deriving from performing under "first-time situation and tough changing conditions". "Learning agility" can be related to the Fluid intelligence factor (Gf) rather

---

3   Father also of the trait tool 16PF , Raymond Cattell wanted to map the "periodic table" of personality and developed this questionnaire in 1949 (restandardized 4 times since, last in 2002). The well known personality psychometric 16PF (16 Personality Factor, Publisher OPP) based on a 16 scale, looks at personality in its entirety, focusing on professional and private life.

than to Crystallized intelligence (Gc). Research shows that the ability of novel problem solving, finding better strategies and adapting to novel situations is an ability deriving from Fluid Intelligence (Gf). The theory of fluid and crystallized general intelligence factors has been examined in regard to array of implications. A distinction has been drawn between a general achievement factor (g) and crystallized intelligence (Gc) factor, both distinct from Fluid Intelligence (Gf) factor. General achievement factor (g) and Crystallized Intelligence (Gf) change their pattern a) with age and b) with culture as to constitute relatively poor predictors of other performances in groups or different ages and heterogeneous subcultures. Cattel's research showed thus the existence of two general ability factors:

1. The first fits the **crystallized ability factor** measured in traditional intelligence tests, while the second is:

2. a **Fluid Intelligence** general ability measured in culture-fair intelligence tests. Meaning that Fluid Intelligence tests are less exposed to cultural biases due to cultural differences.

The following sections will try to cast some light on these different constructs by looking at the work of cognitive psychologists specialized in the neurosciences such as Engle and Unsworth (2007), Vogel (2004, 2005), Tuholski, Laughlin & Conway (1999), Friedman et al (2006), Kane et al (2004); Shelton, Elliott, Hill, Calamia, & Gouvier (2009), Matthews & Hill (2010).

CRYSTALLIZED INTELLIGENCE

A book that retained my attention recently is *"The talent code"* written by David Coyle (2009). His standpoint is that ability can be created and nurtured, it is not a mystical power fixed at birth. He visited and observed talent hotbeds all over the world, be it football schools that provided some of the greatest players, music schools in the US, a Tennis academy in Russia, to demonstrate how the wiring of our brains, according to the latest studies in neurosciences, can be transformed by the way we approach particular tasks. He explains what is really happening when apparently unremarkable people suddenly make a major leap forward and reveals why some teaching methods are so much more effective than others. Above all, he shows how people can achieve full potential if set to train the brain in the right way. Full potential of their Crystallized intelligence abilities, if we want to be more precise.

Improvement in skills and even in reasoning has been reached by training reasoning and rule abstraction. The trainees get better in what they were trained in, and they improve also in other tasks within the range of the trained function, but there is no transfer to other fields. This is what we call Crystallized intelligence. Coyle's book explains the importance of a scientific discovery involving a neural insulator called myelin, which some neurologists now consider as the holy grail of acquiring skill. Every human skills, he explains, whether it's playing baseball or playing Bach, is created by chains of nerve fibers carrying a tiny electrical impulse – basically, a signal traveling through a circuit. Myelin's role is to wrap around those nerve fibers the same way that rubber insulation wraps around a copper wire, making the signal stronger, faster, more precise and preventing the electrical impulses from leaking out. Multiple sclerosis is the disease that destroys myelin, destroys skills, in the advanced stages the ability to walk. In the absence of disease, when we practice a skill, be it a swing in golf or a sonata on the piano, our myelin responds by wrapping layers of insulation around the neural circuit, each new layer adding a bit more skill and speed. The thicker the myelin layer, the better it insulates, and the faster and more accurate our movements and thoughts become. Skill derives from experience and practice. Skill is a cellular insulation that wraps neural circuits and those grow in response to certain signals. As George Bartzokis, a UCLA neurologist and myelin researcher put it: "All skills, all language, all music, all movements, are made of living circuits, and all circuits grow according to certain rules". What David Coyle observed visiting all those talent hotbeds is that those people practice in a very special way. They are engaged in an activity that seems all the time at the edge of their ability, so that they will screw up. Somehow screwing up is making them better. An interesting example he gives in his book is the talent of Brazilian soccer players, that can be measured by the five World Cup victories. The conventional way to explain this kind of concentrated talent is to attribute it to a combination of genes and environment. But there is a problem with this explanation – Brazil did not win anything until the late 1950s. So how does Brazil produce so many great players? The surprising answer is that Brazil has been producing great players since the late fifties because they

The Name of the Game

have trained in a particular way, with a particular tool that improves ball-handling skill faster than anywhere else in the world. They have found a way to increase their learning speed, although they were barely aware of it. It's what Coyle calls deep practice training, and it applies to more than soccer. It applies also to Human resources development practice, as we will see in the fifth chapter. An intriguing way to understand the concept of deep practice is to do the following exercise, taking a few seconds to look at the two lists:

Ocean/Breeze   Bread/B_tter
Leaf/Tree   Music/L_rics
Sweet/Sour   Phone/B_ok
Movie/Actress   Pen_il/Paper

Now, without looking, try to remember as many of the word pairs as you can. From which column do you recall more words? If you are like most people, it won't even be close: you will remember more words from the second column, the one that contains fragments. Studies show (Craik and Lockhardt, 1972 show the cognitive basis for this effect) that you will remember three times as many. When you encountered the words with blank spaces, something imperceptible and profound happened. You stumbled ever so briefly, then figured it out. There was a micro-second of struggle, of effort. That micro-second made the difference. You did not practice harder when looking at the second column, you practiced deeper. This is also the way Brazilian soccer players found a way to practice deeper. Experiences where you are forced to slow down, make errors, and correct them, make you smarter, make you swifter

COGNITIVE POTENTIAL: WHY WE WASTE TALENT

and more precise, often without realizing it. Robert Bjork, the chair of psychology at UCLA has spent most of his career delving into questions of memory and learning and he affirmed: "We think of effortless performance as desirable, but it's really a terrible way to learn". Making mistakes is of crucial importance in the learning process. Simulation exercises can be an answer to this problem; it is what President Franklin Roosevelt decided to apply to combat airmen. They were dying in crashes all the time in the early thirties, in 1934 it became a scandal in the United States. The belief at that time was that good pilots are born, not made. Edwin Link believed in skill development, he developed a training method on a simulator, casualties dropped and seven years later, World War II began and with it the need to transform thousands of unskilled youth into pilots as quickly and safely as possible. That need was answered by ten thousand "Link trainers" simulators, that permitted pilots to practice more deeply, to struggle, stall, make errors and learn from them. Let's go back to Brazil's soccer. How come so many first class players that are bought by the strongest clubs all over Europe are Brazilian? Apart from the fact that they log twenty hours per week training, compared with five hours per week for their British counterparts, a passionate researcher in 1997 saw something he did not expect, a strange game (that became popular all over the world since, called futsal). Coyle reporting the discovery of this researcher described it in the following way: "*It resembled soccer, if soccer were played inside a phone booth and dosed with amphetamines. The ball was half the size but weighed twice as much; it hardly bounced at all. The players trained, not on a vast expanse of grass field, but on a basketball-court*

The Name of the Game

size of concrete, instead of having eleven players they had five or six. In its rhythm the game resembled more to basketball than to soccer: it consisted of an intricate series of quick, controlled passes and nonstop end-to-end action. The game was called futebol de salão." Since the mid-thirties Brazil became obsessed with Futsal and every great Brazilian player played futsal as a kid. How did it happen? One reason lies in the math. Futsal players touch the ball far more often than soccer players – six to eight times more per minute. The smaller, heavier ball demands and rewards more precise handling –Sharp passing is key: the game is all about looking for angles and spaces and working quick combinations with other players.

Coyle writes "*Futsal compresses soccer's essential skills into a small box; it places players inside the deep practice zone, making and correcting errors, constantly generating solutions to vivid problems. Players touching the ball six-hundred time more often learn far faster, without realizing it, than they would in the vast, bouncy expanse of the outdoor game*".

The fact that a targeted and repeated effort can improve skills is not new. What is interesting in Coyle's book is the role of myelin and the role of what he describes as the most effective learning strategy: mistake-focused practice. Struggle, he writes, is not an option, it's a biological requirement. Passion and persistence are key-ingredients of talent, since wrapping myelin around a big circuit requires immense energy and time. It also creates a powerfully convincing illusion: skill once gained, feels utterly natural, as if it's something we have always possessed. This powerful and convincing illusion is an interesting point worth looking into. Fred E. Fiedler published an article titled *"When IQ + experience ≠ performance"* (2001). This article proposes that commonly used methods of selecting leaders and managers, such as résumés of experience and training, tests and interviews, do not offer accurate predictions of future leader performance. It suggests that many current selection practices are based on two flawed assumptions : that greater intelligence (IQ tests) or experience results in better leadership performance; and that the work environment does not impact on how individuals use their abilities and skills. Fiedler argues with reference to representative studies, that experienced leaders performed substantially less well than inexperienced leaders when stress was low. The assumption Fiedler makes is a possible interference between intelligence and experience. One is that people with high intelligence tend to trust their problem-solving abilities and distrust "hunch intuition", they get caught in the trap of previous situations that resemble the problem they are facing. They think "we have done this before and we know what to do" and become impatient with time consuming discussions. This means falling into habit, custom and what can be called crystallized knowledge. Crystallized intelligence (not Fluid intelligence) notions that are the product of past experiences become the default solution. Habit becomes the answer. We do not agree with Fiedler's assumption that intelligence (fluid intelligence) and experience interfere with each other "because we cannot simultaneously think of new solutions for solving problems while automatically responding on the basis of past experience". This disagreement will be explained in the following section. It's not a matter of interference, it's a matter of being able to ignore interference, ignore past experience and habit and focus on finding new strategies to solve the new situation.

FLUID INTELLIGENCE (Gf)

Fluid intelligence is considered as the ability to reason and to solve problems that influence learning in everyday life in both professional and educational settings. Although there are some articles that sustain the possibility of enhancing fluid intelligence by training, there is very little evidence that this is possible. You can develop skills and score slightly higher in the fluid intelligence tests, by doing them over and over again, but this does not enhance your fluid intelligence ability factor, it is apparently "immune to training". What makes fluid intelligence "fluid" is that it is transferable, meaning that it can be transferred to other domains (Perring, Hollenstein, Oelhafen, 2009). One aspect that is worth emphasizing however, is that Fluid intelligence (Gf), being related to other forms of intelligence is not completely determined by heredity factors. Behavioral interventions, such as schooling and other factors have markedly positive influences.

In the past decade, cognitive scientists have entertained the notion that "working memory capacity" (WMC) is the "factor X" that underlies individual differences in general intelligence (or Spearman's g factor). But recent research (differential, experimental and neuroimaging research projects) has uncovered important details about the information-processing requirements of WMC tasks and the fact that Fluid intelligence (Gf) seems to be a major dimension of individual differences and refers to:

- reasoning and
- novel problem-solving ability.

Cognitively, fluid intelligence is thought to be related to meta-cognition (knowing about and reflecting upon one's own ongoing mental process) and to working memory (WM).

Working memory has been defined as a brain system to temporarily store and manipulate information (Smith & Jonides, 1999) One definition of WMC is "*the active maintenance of domain-specific information plus domain general attentional- or 'executive control of ongoing processes despite interference*" (Gray, Chabris and Braver in Nature, 2003). Fluid intelligence (Gf) is involved in reasoning and when complex relationships have to be perceived and used to find solution for new problems. Fluid intelligence and WMC are closely related factors and can be measured by various tests (N-back task, Raven Multimatrices Test…etc). Those tests, such as the 3-back task, "*measure the ability to overcome interference that would otherwise disrupt performance by compromising tasks goals or information held active in working memory*" (Shelton and al., American Psychological Association, 2010). Understanding the nature of this relationship is critical in determining why working memory (WM) is especially useful in predicting how well people can reason and adapt to an increasingly complex environment and novel problem solving situations.

The Name of the Game

On a neural level, it has been argued that both WM and Gf are based on overlapping brain areas, in particular dorsolateral prefrontal cortex (Kane & Engle, 2002) and parietal areas. Neuroimaging permitted us to see how these areas are activated during tests. Patients with frontal lobe lesions permitted us to better understand the functions of those factors and gave valuable information about behaviors and activities linked to those brain regions, where research showed impairments in measures of Fluid intelligence -or goal directed behavior (Duncan, Burgess & Emslie, 1995), while knowledge-based crystallized intelligence was less affected. *"That's why Working memory capacity plays an important role in guiding behavior. Thus understanding how WM works and how it interacts with attentional mechanisms, reflects a fundamental question in cognitive neurosciences"* (Luria & Vogel 2011).

Working memory capacity might thus be relevant when assessing talent. Working memory tasks require adequate processing of two simultaneous tasks, such as storing (research showed that WM storage capacity = ≤ 4 items[4]), manipulating information at the same time and the inhibition (ignoring) of irrelevant information are the most important candidates for the task construction (the WM test).

---

[4] There is a test called Visual-array comparison task, where an array of colored squares is presented briefly, followed by an inter-stimulus interval, followed by a second array that is identical or similar to the first. One square in the second array is marked by a circle, and if the two arrays were different, the difference was in the color of the encircled square. The key factor is the number of squares presented in the arrays. When the array is small (≤4) same/different judgments are very accurate. However, accuracy deteriorates when the array size is greater than 4, suggesting that approximately 4 independent locations can be actively maintained in Working Memory without the aid of a grouping or other strategy. This task provides an estimate of maximum WMC.

COGNITIVE POTENTIAL: WHY WE WASTE TALENT

Cattell assumed that there are nine variables that consist of five Thurston Primary abilities – *Verbal, Spatial, Reasoning, Number and Fluency* – and four subtests that are more **culture-fair**:

- *Perceptual series,*
- *Perceptual classification,*
- *Matrices and*
- *Typology.*

The first primary abilities, with exception of spatial and fluency performances, should load on crystallized ability factor, while the culture-fair subtests, being purely perceptual **should load only a fluid general ability factor**. One of the standard measures to assess Fluid Intelligence (or the fluid ability factor) is the *Raven's Advanced Progressive Matrices*. Another widely used test to probe WM is the three-back task (N-back task). In one version of this test, participants view a series of stimuli that are either all words or all faces or geometrical figures for a given scanning (MRI) run, with a new stimulus item appearing every 2-5 seconds. Participants are instructed to indicate as quickly and accurately as possible whether each stimulus *matched or did not match the stimulus seen three items previously,* using two response buttons (in some cases just answering if the person detects an n-3 repeate, so there is no need to respond when this is not the case) . The three-back match requires a 'target response'; in the sequence **A-B-C-A** the second A is a target. In case there is A-B-**A**-A, the second A is called a "lure" (non-target trial) they are interferences that demand a higher level of control.

The Name of the Game

There are two-back, four-back and five-back tests that can use words, geometrical figures, or faces. A lure item can be easily confused with a target because the mere fact that it was seen recently is typically far more salient than its precise position within the temporal sequence of recent stimuli. Lure trials should require additional attentional control to overcome the tendency to make a target response merely on the basis of recency. These tests are performed under the MRI and neural imaging shows the parts of the brain that are mostly involved in this activity (Lateral Prefrontal Cortex LPFC). Fluid intelligence differences in brain activity emerged almost exclusively on working memory trials with high interference, those that scored higher were those that maintained control despite interference, that ignored lures protecting goals, or other information held actively in mind, from such interferences. In other words, those that score higher in WMC tasks have an ability to maintain access to information and goals in the face of distraction, interference, and shifts of conscious focus. People with lower WMC are less able than people with higher WMC to sustain goal-directed thought and behavior in the face of competition from environmental and mental events (Kane & al, Psychological Science, 18, 2007, p.617). People with higher Fluid Intelligence (measured through WM tests as N-back, Raven's Advanced Progressive Matrices[5],RSPAN[6]

---
5 The Raven's Progressive Matrices Test, a test that previously thought to be a relatively pure measure of psychometric g and findings showed that I is highly dependent on fluid cognition (and integrity of the Prefrontal Cortex), if you want to test go: http://www.raventest.net/raven-test.html.
6 In the reading span "RSPAN task" the subject might memorize short lists of letters, with each letter preceded by an unrelated sentence to judge for meaningfulness.

and OSPAN[7]) on average, outperform those with lower WMC on attention tasks requiring the active maintenance of novel goals in order to override habitual responding (Kane, Bleckley, Conway & Engle 2001). Low-WMC subjects seem to periodically lose focus on their goals, or "zone out" (Shooler, Richle, & Halpern 2004) when executive control is challenged. Recent studies showed that WMC tasks correlate strongly with a wide range of cognitive abilities; with Gf in particular they share substantial variance (Conway, Kane& Engle 2003; Kane, Conway, Hambrick, 2005). In short, people with lower WMC show "*poorer control over thought and action than do those with higher WMC by failing more often to prevent or recover from prepotent responses and by showing slower and less flexible allocation of visual attention to objects in space*" (Kane & al. 2005). There is thus a distinction between tasks that require storage and retrieval (Gc) versus those that require storage and some form of processing (Gf). Working in demanding business environments, responding to challenging first-time situations, in face of interference and stress requires high-Gf capacities. How do neural measures reveal individual differences in controlling access to working memory? Vogel et al. (Nature, 2005) carried out a stunning experiment. They developed a visual short-term memory test, since visual memory has a very limited capacity, it can maintain only three to four objects simultaneously. They showed that high capacity individuals are much more

---

7   In an operation span « OSPAN task » each letter is preceded by an equation to verify. The insertion of secondary tasks between memory items means that subjects are required to recall information that is periodically unattended (Barouillet, Bernadin and Camos, 2004) and vulnerable to pro-active interference.

efficient at representing only the relevant items than low capacity individuals, who inefficiently retain information about the irrelevant items present in the display. Vogel et al. recorded event-related potentials from healthy young adults while they performed a visual memory task in which it was necessary to remember selectively only a few relevant items from within an array (ex. an array of red rectangles and blue rectangles). In each trial they were presented with a brief bilateral array of colored rectangles of varying orientations and were asked to remember the orientations of only the red items in either the left or right hemi-field (indicated by the arrows). Subjects reported whether the red items in the two arrays were identical or not, by pressing one of two buttons. In the third trial, two red items were presented with two blue items in each hemi-field. On the remaining trials, arrays of either two red items or four red items alone were presented. They measured a special wave-form named CDA (Contralateral Delay Activity), known to monitor the number of objects maintained in visual WM. This enabled Vogel et al. to observe directly whether the subjects could exclude the irrelevant blue items from being stored in visual memory. If you look below in the figure, you will notice that the amplitude of the CDA waves increases significantly as the number of representations being held in memory increases. This limit is measured as a difference in amplitude between an array of four items and an array of two items.

COGNITIVE POTENTIAL: WHY WE WASTE TALENT

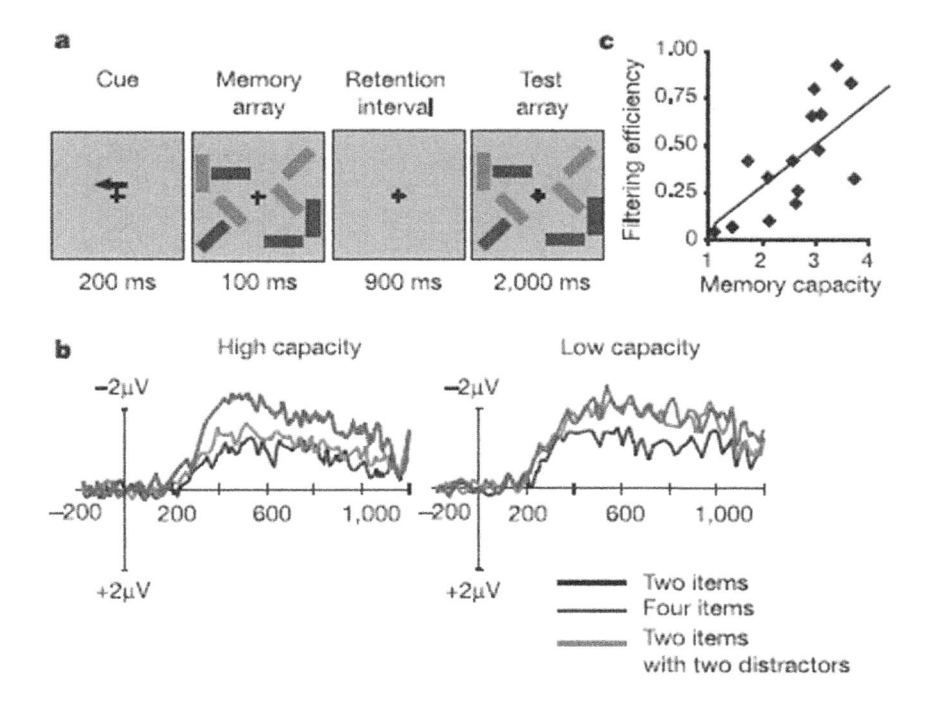

a

Cue	Memory array	Retention interval	Test array
200 ms	100 ms	900 ms	2,000 ms

c

Filtering efficiency vs Memory capacity (1–4); scatter with positive trend, values 0 to 1.00.

b

High capacity / Low capacity ERP waveforms, −2μV to +2μV, time −200 to 1,000 ms.

— Two items
— Four items
— Two items with two distractors

Low capacity individuals show a smaller difference than high capacity individuals, indicating that an array of two items consumes a larger proportion of available memory capacity in low capacity individuals. Furthermore, if an individual was perfectly efficient at remembering only the red items and excluding the blue items from memory, then the wave amplitude should be equivalent to that observed when two red items were presented alone. In contrast, if an individual was perfectly inefficient at excluding blue items, all four of the items in the array (two red and two blue) would be stored in memory resulting in an amplitude equal to that when four red items alone were presented. Memory capacity varies considerably across individuals and this experiment indicated that low capacity subjects are highly inefficient at excluding irrelevant information by exerting effective control over any aspect of working memory functioning.

LEARNING AGILITY

Going now back to "learning agility", it has often been cited by HR Directors during the interviews and it appears often in leadership publications as key-factor that enables high-potential identification. *Learning agility* is first found in two studies at the Center for Creative Leadership (McCall, Lombardo and Morrison 1998, Morrison, White and Van Velsor 1992) and since 2002 in various consulting company's potential models. They found that if people have certain powerful on-the-job experiences and learn from them, that this is a strong predictor of long-term success. They noticed that successful executives had a strong and similar pattern of learning from key job assignments. But some derailed executives had been successful for many years and were suddenly blocked to new learning. Either people quit learning or they think that their experience will give answers to any given situation. They relied on what had gotten them to where they were. Lombardo and Eichinger (2002) refer to this behavior as "non-learning pattern". Rather than non-learning pattern, they got locked into habit and crystallized behavioral patterns. To this "learning agility" factor they added another measurement of potential "*that strengthens it, that is willingness and ability to learn new competencies in order to perform under first-time, tough different conditions*" (Lombardo and Eichinger 2002, p.4). Here the authors mixed up Gc factor, which is the ability to learn specific competencies (an exercise associated to motivation and effort), with Gf factor, which is to perform under first-time conditions, as required in problem solving in new situations. Lombardo and al. created a questionnaire managers can use to assist in nominating high-potentials with greater ease and accuracy. The questionnaire is based on a series of studies conducted at CCL that tried to identify items that were either explicitly learning oriented or required learning in order to perform under first-time conditions. This calls to mind strongly the Fluid intelligence factor, even though the authors never refer to the cognitive psychology articles discussed above. As a result of these studies they quote four factors that describe different facets of learning agility that mix Gf factor, Gc factor and Emotional intelligence factors :

1. **People agility**: describes people who know themselves well, learn from experience, treat others constructively, and are cool and resilient under the pressure of change;

2. **Result agility**: describes people who get results under tough conditions, inspire others to perform beyond normal, and exhibit the sort of presence that builds confidence in others;

3. **Mental agility**: describes people who think through problems from a fresh point of view and are comfortable with complexity, ambiguity and explaining their thinking to others;

4. **Change agility**: describes people who are curious, have a passion for ideas, like to experiment with test cases, and engage in skill building activities.

The Name of the Game

Lombardo and Eichinger conclude that each of these factors was significantly associated with being considered a high potential and staying out of trouble. Beyond the data itself, they gave two insights into the "learning agile". The first is that they describe them as people that seem to be driven to learn as a value in itself (in other terms they are growth-mindset people). The second point was about 'staying out of trouble', meaning that they are self-aware and know their limits and learn from their mistakes (growth-mindset people are much more precise when it comes to self-assessment).

As an interviewed Senior HR Director said: "*Emotional intelligence is what defines the bottom line of High-potentials. If you have all the rest, all cognitive abilities including results, and you score low on this variable there isn't much hope in our organization*".

The fact that cognitive, psychometric, genetic and neuroimaging studies are converging and give rise to a mechanistic model of intelligence has profound implications on ethics implying a trait-like quality of intelligence. Conceptions of mental ability have far-reaching implications for theories of human nature. The implications for society are nothing short of "incendiary", the fear is not entirely irrational – i.e. a group is stereotyped as being of lower intelligence (Gray and Thompson, 2004). Individuals differ from one another in their ability to understand complex ideas, to adapt effectively to the environment, to learn from experience, to engage in various forms of reasoning, to overcome obstacles using thought. Although these individual differences can be substantial, they are never entirely consistent: a given person's intellectual performance will vary on different occasions, in different domains, as when judged by different criteria. MRI neuroimaging shows that negative emotions, sadness, depression, high levels of negative stress imply a decreased cognitive ability. Such reciprocal interconnectivity of emotion and cognition in the brain is highly consistent with the idea that fluid cognitive functioning is goal directed. Clancy Blair writes "Working memory and cognitive control processes are utilized in the service of specific goal related to problem solving and learning. However, at high levels of emotional arousal, fluid cognitive functions become inhibited, and impairments in the control of attention, working memory, and inhibitory control are more likely to occur[8]" (Blair, 2006, p.117). Research shows that there is no potential 'categorical imperative'. You can score high in working memory and fluid intelligence, have great people skills and EQ, however an unhealthy work environment will impact your capacities. Research shows that negative stress, a bad boss as well as depression can disrupt cognitive capacity and bring impairments to executive control and working memory capacity. A positive, supportive and growth oriented work environment can thus be crucial for unleashing potential and preserve "learning agility".

---

[8] Individuals sustaining damage to PFC results in difficulty in regulation of emotion and is associated with anomalous decision-making in response to information regarding for example the likely reward or penalty associated with a given choice (Bechara and al., 1999)

Chapter 4

POTENTIAL WHAT FOR? AN INTEGRATED MODEL

HIGH POTENTIAL QUALITIES AND TRAITS

What does a high-potential look like? By what means can we assess potential? By looking for what traits can we identify high-potential employees? If we take a quick glimpse at history we can refer to the work of Frederic Taylor at the beginning of the twentieth century. Taylorist efficiency experts swept the world of work analyzing the most mechanically efficient moves a worker's body could make. The measure of human work, was the machine. On the heels of Taylorism, as we mentioned already quoting Dweck, came another standard of evaluation: IQ. The correct measure of excellence was the cognitive abilities of the human mind. Then with the rise of Freudian and Jungian thinking, another wave of scholars argued that in addition to IQ, personality was an ingredient in excellence. By the 1960s, personality tests and typologies – such as the MBTI – were part of the standard measurement of potential. The problem was that many of the personality tests had been designed for completely different reasons, such as diagnosing psychological disorders. They were poor predictors of how people could perform in their jobs. Now they became a developmental tool, a way to discover and be more conscious of one's preferences. Just like personality tests, also IQ tests showed they were not infallible: people with high IQ often performed poorly, while those with lower IQ did extremely well. McClelland's paper of 1973 we quoted earlier "Testing for Competence rather than intelligence" shifted the terms of the debate. He argued that traditional academic performance, school grades and IQ did not predict how well people would perform on the job or whether they would succeed. He proposed that a set of specific competencies including *empathy, self-discipline (self-control) and initiative* distinguished the most successful if compared to those who were merely good. His paper was a milestone to an entirely new approach to the measure of excellence. A measurement that assesses *people's competencies in terms of a specific job they are doing*. Goleman (1998) defines a "competence" in this tradition as a personal trait or set of habits that lead to a more effective or superior job performance – in other words, is an ability that adds clear economic value to the efforts of a person on the job. McClelland insight has inspired research over the past 30 years. In all findings, a common core of personal and social abilities has proven to be the key ingredient in people's success: emotional intelligence. This shift is also perceived in an organizational perspective. Over the years, the nature of organizational talent has changed (Sears, 2003) from a focus on division of labor distinctions to an evaluation of strategic contributions to the organization. Sears suggests that talent is "knowledge", understood as a "competitive advantage" and that it is shaped by what customers value.

Silzer and Church's study (2009) aims to provide a review and synthesis of the variables that have been used across the different fields of practice and research to identify potential in individuals and discuss the limits of this exercise. They say the approach they have taken in this article to identify high-potential talent does not include individuals being assessed for an immediate next leadership role for a specific job. They have focused on potential with a longer planning horizon in an organization (eg. for general management roles in the future). Even though we don't agree with this approach since it's too generic and tends to oversimplify reality according to what we can now call a linear-system dynamic, it's nonetheless interesting to look at all those key-variables that are supposed to define high-potential. As part of the increasing strategic role of human resources in business strategy, organizations are focusing on identifying and developing talent in order to achieve business objectives. One key component of this effort involves identifying the talent that already exists in the organization. In order to identify talent and help people improve current performance there are assessment tools or assessment reviews that appraise the current status and give feedback on how to develop skills and competencies for the current or for the next position. Potential as "something that can be developed and become actual" (Merriam-Webster, Inc. 2002). An interesting linguistic observation shows that many leaders, managers and HR professionals view this concept of potential as an inherent

The Name of the Game

individual capability (either you have it or you don't), as an innate trait or natural capability. Some consulting firms have asserted that potential factors "are extremely difficult to develop" (Rogers and Smith, 2007). Some organizations use the term generically: *he or she is a high-potential individual.* In this case potential is not defined and it becomes a category, which would suggest that it can be identified and measured independently of the context and as something immutable across situations. "Much like general intelligence" write Silzer and Church. This approach is a typical fixed-mindset approach. Concerning the comparison to "general intelligence", we will see it is misleading, it's oversimplifying reality. It's true that not everybody will become Beethoven, Mozart or Steve Jobs. However, what we can call an "ignition" process, what can unleash potential, depends upon one's motivation, ambition and drive as well as upon the organizational environment and specific context. No matter how highly endowed you are with intelligence and natural gifts, if you are not motivated, if you work in a hostile or unsupportive environment all this potential, all those gifts won't be of much use. A survey of American employers led by the Harris Education Research Council (1991) reveals that more than half the people who work for the companies lack the motivation to keep learning and improving in their job. Given how much emphasis schools and admissions test put on IQ, it is surprising that IQ alone explains little about how well people perform and achieve in life. When IQ scores are correlated with how well people perform in their careers, the highest estimate of how much difference IQ accounts for is about 25 percent (F.L.Schmidt and J.B. Hunter, Psychological

POTENTIAL WHAT FOR? AN INTEGRATED MODEL

American Psychologist 36, 1981). A careful analysis, though, suggests a more accurate figure that may be no higher than 10 percent, and perhaps as low than 4 percent (Robert Sternberg, 1996; D. Goleman 1998). Having in mind Cattell's article on crystallized and fluid intelligence we know why. That means that what you have learned in school is just a threshold competence; it's what you need to get into the field, but it does not make you a top performer or a star. It's the "emotional intelligence abilities that matter more for superior performance" says Lyle Spencer Jr, Director of research and technology worldwide and co-founder of what is now the Hay Group, the consulting firm McClelland started. Claudio Fernandez-Arraoz, in charge of executive searches throughout Latin America from Egon Zehnder Intenational's Buenos Aires office, compared 227 highly successful executives with 23 who failed in their jobs. He found that the managers who failed were almost always high in expertise and IQ. If they measured IQ, we know that they measured the wrong factor: Crystallized intelligence (Gc ability factor). In every case their fatal weakness was in emotional intelligence – arrogance, overeliance on brainpower or experience, inability to adapt to the occasionally disorienting economic shift in that region, and disdain for collaboration and team-work (1997). As we said above, IQ isn't enough to assure high performance. If we lack motivation we won't do much with our cognitive capabilities. Goleman affirms (1998) that flow is the ultimate motivator. Activities we love draw us in because we get into flow as we pursue them, in other words, intrinsic motivation. Flow offers a radical alternative to the widely held ideas about what motivates people at work. If we think of McClelland's achievement motivation theory and power motives and managerial performance (McClelland, 1975), the flow offers a more developmental approach. We won't enter further into the details of McClelland's theory, but we will refer to it again later when discussing managerial competencies and in particular leadership styles. Launching the competency movement, McClelland did not propose a theory of human competence or performance, but rather a procedure for studying such factors as motives, traits, self-concepts, knowledge, and skills as they interact to produce superior as opposed to average performance. This competency framework gave rise to many derivatives over the years and a substantial consulting industry as well. Many consulting firms have developed their own model of key-competencies using this framework, such as Hay Group (2006, 2008), Hewitt Associates (2008), Hogan Assessment Systems (Hogan, 2009), Corporate Leadership Council (CLC, 2005), Egon Zehnder Int. (Competencies Model 2000, High Potential Module 2011), McCall (McCall 1998), MDA Leadership Consulting (Barnett, 2008), Personnel Decisions (Peterson & Erdahl, 2007) among many others. We will have a close look at those variables for potential assessment discussing and comparing the different models and reporting the recent comparative study published by Silzer and Church. *The Pearls and Perils of identifying Potential (2009)*. McClelland associates motivational patterns with leadership styles, scaling performance according to stages of "maturity". In the Egon Zehnder Potential assessment module motives are embedded within the other dimensions, they emerge through cognitive variables (insight, curiosity, ...)

and leadership variables (ability to engage others, motivating, showing resilience and determination facing adversity, drive..). Silzer and Church in their paper reported what they call the "current model of potential", which is declined in six variables as shown below, having each key-themes:

Cognitive	Personality	Learning	Leadership	Motivation	Performance
Conceptual/ strategic thinking, breath of thinking	Interpersonal skills, sociability	Adaptability, flexibility	Leadership capabilities, managing and empowering people,	Drive, energy, engagement, tenacity	Performance track record, Leadership experience
Intellect, cognitive ability	Dominance Maturity, stability, resilience	Learning orientation, interest in learning	Developing others,	Aspiration, drive for advancement, ambition,	
Dealing with complexity/ ambiguity		Openness to feedback	Influencing, inspiring, challenging the status quo, change management	career drive, organizational commitment Result orientation, risk taking	

Silzer and Church report a significant mind shift from short-term selection to long-term prediction in the past few years. Organizations became more and more interested in a prediction process that might predict 3 to 10 years ahead. The prediction does not want to match an individual to a specific position and responsibilities, but rather to predict how much potential an individual has, with additional growth and development, to be a candidate in the future for a group of senior executive positions. We shall keep in mind that both the individual and the future position are likely to change and evolve over the years before promotion into a specific role is considered. I am sceptical when I hear about this growing interest in identifying those individuals who have the most potential to be effective in higher level organizational roles without defining for what role they are thought for.. One of the dimensions the potential construct seems to be always measured against is leadership and management skills. To step up towards higher senior executive position leadership seems to be omnipresent. However, very recently, by interviewing HR Directors of large listed organizations we witnessed a new kind of high potential profile being defined: expert high potential. This category of high-potential needs collaborative skills more than leadership, and is a reference in technical skills. If we think of highly specialized companies in the nuclear sector or construction, those highly specialized experts are a strategic reference and resource for the future success of the organization. I interviewed a Head of Human Resources who worked for three companies in different business sectors. John affirmed that in his point of view "*the profile of high-potentials depends also upon the nature of the business*". Interviewing another senior HR Director of a large German organization, I discovered they don't have high-potential lists. They are convinced that it's of the utmost importance to keep a talent management approach and perspective for the sake of equity in the organization, avoiding any kind of elitism. The senior HR Director I interviewed in his previous position within another listed company, worked for a company that had high-potential lists and communicated openly about the identified few. He affirmed that this practice gave rise to quite a few negative effects. He witnessed many deviations and perils in this approach. It created a division between the potential "haves" and the "have-nots" (i.e. those determined to have lower potential). This division runs the risk of disengaging the non-high-potentials individuals, which is arguably the majority of the employee population in most organizations which counts for 85-90 percent of the workforce. We found that the most common level of high-potential employees within an organization is of around 5-10 percent of total population, in some organization up to 20 percent and in others as low as 1 percent, data that is confirmed by DeLong and Vijayaraghavan (2003). Furthermore, this HR Director argued that the former company he worked for and left in 2009, identified in 2000 ten exceptionally smart young executives who were informed that they were high-potentials. They were put on a fast track career path and worked together on strategic projects. What happened is that as soon as one of their expectations was frustrated, a promotion they were expecting wasn't announced at the time they expected, a sign of gratitude wasn't granted, or a negative feedback on a particular dimension was pronounced, they left the company. Of 10 stars hired in 2000 only two stayed with the company. That's why John is now convinced that a talent management approach is healthier than a high-potential management approach. What struck me in his discourse, compared to many other interviews I carried out, where organizations had a high-potential program, was that he defined talent in organizations as a *collective* and not an individual dimension. He said: "*What I retain from my 25 years experience is that it's much easier to spoil talent than to make it grow and emerge*", explaining that many programs have good intentions, but end up spoiling their resources by choosing certain policies and practices that are in his point of view risky and often counter-productive. Another HR Director stressed the importance of the individual high-potential dimension in a very decentralized organization, where the achievement of one person can make a difference in small subsidiaries in emerging countries for example. The <u>business defines priorities</u>.

The first and most common issue with potential in organizations is that as a construct it is poorly defined.

Just to quote a few recent papers : *High potentials as high-learners* (Michael M. Lombardo and R.W.Eichinger for Lominger the Leadership architects than published in Human Resource Management, 2000, vol.39), or *Discover the DNA of Future CEOs* (Korn Ferry/ Whitehead Mann (2008), or *Creating People Advantage* (BCG, 2011). This is probably why the high-potential model developed by the Corporate Leadership Council (2005) is one of the most widely cited models by corporations. Another observation is that much of the research that does exist is centered on validating a specific assessment tool or model and not on providing a comprehensive comparison of approaches to identifying high potentials. Being poorly defined, most organizations base their definition of potential solely on the perceived degree of potential for vertical movement to a specific level in the organization within a given time span. Most of the time (almost 90 percent of the organizations we consulted) we observed that it's a two level up movement within a time span of 2-5 years. This impression is confirmed by statistical data: in a survey of 252 organizations, led by the Corporate Leadership Council (2005), 47% of them defined high potentials based on their ability to advance two to four levels, and another 26 percent of the organizations planned to move in this direction soon. Given that the definition is often poor makes us turn to some of the ways that the construct of potential and potential identification are misused in organizations. We already discussed the nine-box grid and the potential/performance paradox, where companies rely almost exclusively on past performance in identifying potential, which is a clear problem as we discussed earlier, because past performance is unlikely to accurately predict successful future behavior in significantly different situations. Other authors base potential on "certain leadership competencies or even on strategically needed functional knowledge, which is clearly better than the smoke-filled-room assessment practices of the past" (McCall, 1998). However, another limitation as Silzer and Church note, is that even when a formal definition is present in an organization, it will not be effectively used if there is not a shared mind-set, a shared structured approach regarding potential identification and assessment. There is always a tendency for managers and leaders to use the implicit model that they have in their mind, given that each of us has our own definition of what a high-potential should look like (Sloan, 2001). This evokes the problem we already discussed in the previous chapter of who's assessing potential and how, of whether managers are trained in using assessment tools or not. One of the strengths of Egon Zehnder and a few other consulting firms is that they carry out assessments, but also train clients to use the assessment tools. Clients, be it managers or HR professionals receive accreditation to use specific assessment tools, so that they can share a more reliable and explicit measurement scale. Another misuse of potential concerns high-potential identification programs that are conceived as a "stand-alone" effort and not integrated within the business strategy, with other ongoing programs. We noticed this in companies where age is the only reference in career management. They wanted to modernize their talent management approach and decided to create a high-potential talent pool, however nothing in terms of HR practices supported this new talent pool. High-potentials were informed of being selected, but figured out within a couple of years that nothing really changed in terms of internal staffing, nor in terms of other developmental programs or succession planning. The old model kept its course and age and seniority within the company remained the main reference in career evolution. The high-potential policy had little impact on the organization and high-potentials began questioning within months what it was all about. There is little point in differentiating talent by potential if that information is not going to be used independently for decision-making. Yet some organizations continue to promote individuals based on performance, while actually referring to potential because it is "easier to justify in the short term" (Bunker Kam & Ting, 2002). Some scholars noticing the perils and negative impact of officially telling high-potentials their status within organizations, have suggested making greater use of the "B" players, also called the *pillars*. They assume that B- players may be more stable and committed employees overall than "A" players, who might be more likely to move to another company given their often higher career ambitions. We interviewed

POTENTIAL WHAT FOR? AN INTEGRATED MODEL

a European Head of Talent Development working in the pharmaceutical sector, that decided a few years ago to always "couple" pillars and high-potential employees. For example if they decided to promote a high-potential to a position of Country Manager, they sustained this risky bet with a "pillar" employee, who was proposed the country CFO position. This was working tremendously well, she stated, also because her organization did not communicate who was a high-potential. Another Group HR Director within the Financial Services Sector affirmed that the "talent war" trend is a dangerous way of perceiving the current situation, since "it makes people ignore the importance of pillars within the organization" by giving too much importance to few individuals. As if talent should fall as a mature fruit from a tree, without the need for nurturing, growth, development and effort. When I read articles like "Tales from the Talent War" or "The war for Talent" (McKinsey) as I already mentioned in this paper, I think about the negative impact of this metaphor. There are a few stars, a narrow elite for whom it's worth battling for, for whom leaders go "down in the trenches", while the rest aren't really worth a second glance. It's an elitist approach organizations should seriously consider before applying. If companies don't communicate about potential, they are absolutely free to identify it and nurture it, without taking unnecessary risks and creating an elitist culture.

When we speak about high-potential identification: What are we trying to predict? There are several common characteristics of high potential talent identification efforts in organizations :

The Name of the Game

- *To identify individuals with the potential to be effective in broader roles at least several career levels into the future, beyond the next promotion*

- *To identify individuals earlier in their career (those who are sometimes labeled in organizations as "diamond in the rough") who might have long term potential.*

In discussing high-potential talent, Silzer and Church (2009) note the target roles were moved further into the future, and the identification period was moved to earlier career stages in an attempt to plan for and build talent for the long-term needs of the organization. The point is whether we have to systematically ask the question "potential what for?" or whether there are common components of the high-potential construct across all sectors, organizations and groups that enable recognition. Something that might resemble to Kant's approach to morality: what is it that makes these schemes moral? What form must a precept have if it is to be recognized as a moral percept? Kant approaches this question from an initial assertion that nothing is unconditionally good – except good will. Health, wealth, intellect, are good only insofar as they are used well. The test of a genuine moral imperative is that I can universalize it – that is, that I can will that it should be a universal law. The test consists in asking the question : "Can I consistently will that this precept should be universally acknowledged and acted upon?". This is what Kant calls a categorical imperative (Alasdair MacIntyre, Routledge 1995). In calling them categorical imperatives, Kant contrasts them with hypothetical imperatives. A hypothetical imperative is of the form "you ought to do such and such if….".

POTENTIAL WHAT FOR? AN INTEGRATED MODEL

The *if* may introduce either of two types of condition. There are hypothetical imperatives of skill –"you ought to do such and such if you wish to produce this sort of result" (prevention goal); and hypothetical imperatives of prudence – "you ought to do such and such if you wish to be happy (or for your advantage)" (promotion goals). The categorical imperative is limited by no conditions. What we will try to define is whether we can find the high-potential categorical imperative. Those that are universal, that are not limited by sector, or other kind of condition, the core components of potential.

THE FOUNDATIONAL DIMENSION

Let's start with those dimensions or traits that are more difficult to change. We can call them foundational traits. I would personally include:

- motives and
- cognitive skills. (Fluid Intelligence)

Concerning motives we will make a comparative analysis in this chapter. Concerning cognitive skills, the second foundational trait we refer to Gf. Crystallized intelligence, specific knowledge, specific competencies, abilities can be expanded and improved throughout our life; fluid intelligence, on the other hand, is innate and until now there has been no evidence that it can be further developed by training or exercise. If we look at the comparative table of current models of potential, under cognitive and motives we see the following variables or dimensions listed:

The Name of the Game

	COGNITIVE	MOTIVES
Corporate Leadership Council (2005)	• Cognitive agility	• Aspiration • Engagement
MDA Leadership Consulting (Barnett, 2008)	• Cognitive ability	• Drive • Organizational commitment
Egon Zehnder Int.(2011)	• Derives insight (many variables contained: strategic orientation, pattern & concept think, cause & effect thinking, IQ…	• Motives are embedded in the potential assessment module
Hewitt Associates (Hewitt, 2008)	• Look beyond scope	• Upward motivation
Hogan Assessment Systems (Hogan, 2009)	• Strategic reasoning • Tactical problem solving • Judgement	• Operational excellence • Results orientation • Tenacity
McCall (McCall, 1998)	• Insightful	• Committed to impact • Courage to take risks

Corporate Survey – 20 companies (Silzer & Church, 2009)	• Intellect/ cognitive skills • Handle ambiguity/ complexity	• Career drive • Commitment to company
Our Survey	• Cognitive skills (fluid intelligence) • Learning agility • Adaptability, flexibility	• Energy, drive • Engagement/ Commitment • Ambition (impact)

(Silzer & Church, 2009, pp.392-397)

MOTIVES

If we compare Hogan's model with McCall's model just looking at motives that should drive high-potentials and through which we should be able to identify them, we can notice quite a different approach. Hogan, setting "operational excellence" and "result orientation" as main reference, creates a validation focus. Validation in other words implies a "be-good" approach. McCall's motivational focus is "Committed to impact" and "courage to take risks". For operational excellence you have to be *better than the others*, it's validation you are seeking. "Committed to impact" and "courage to take risks" means on the other hand to expose yourself, to take risks, to deal with complexity and ambiguity. It does not suppose a validation focus. Commitment is a long term focus that implies to striving

The Name of the Game

for something, trying to get better and better. It resembles more a "get better" focus, more than Hewitt's "upward motivation" trait at least, or Hogan's "result orientation". Using Hogan's model we are looking for good soldiers, using McCall's model we are rather looking for good leaders. Before choosing the model we want to apply, we should ask ourselves the question: *what kind of high-potentials are we looking for?* What is the game we want them to play? Good soldiers or more entrepreneurial oriented leaders? People who need constant validation and feel reassured when they achieve results that were set for them, trying to look smarter than others? Or are we looking for people that focus on getting better, that are ready to take risks and expose themselves? It's not just about having the intelligence, the cognitive skills, intellectual capabilities and the right competencies and a track record of outstanding performance. If you don't know what kind of motives to look for when assessing potential, those that move your organization forward in the "right direction", what's the meaning of the exercise?

When assessed, we found sometimes executives that did not take any pleasure from their work and position. Their results were average and when the topic was raised during feed-back they acknowledged that the position did not correspond to what they wanted for themselves, even if it was "good" in terms of status and career path. Often another position corresponded much better to their wishes and once they were conscious of the stalemate they were in, they asked to change and were offered a position that better suited them. *Motives* and *emotions* have the same Latin root: motere. It means "to move". Emotions are literally, what move us to pursue our goals; they fuel our motivation, they permit "ignition" (D.Coyle, 2007). As Goleman writes "Gı work starts with great feelings. Traditional incentives miss the point when it comes to getting people to perform at their absolute best. To <u>reach the top rung, people must love what they do and find pleasure in doing it</u>". If we look at how our brain works we find something quite surprising. J. Hamilton et al., in their paper "Intrinsic enjoyment and boredom coping scales: validation with Personality, Evoked Potential and Attention Measures" (Personality and Individual differences 5,1984) discovered that flow poses a neural paradox : we can be engaged in an exceptionally demanding task, and yet our brain is operating with a minimal level of activity or expenditure of energy. The reasons seems to be that when we are bored and apathetic, or anxious, our brain activity is diffused; the brain itself is at a high level of activation, albeit poorly focused, "with brain cells firing in far-flung and irrelevant ways. But during flow, the brain appears efficient and precise in its patters of firing" (in D.Goleman, 1998). We all have strengths and weaknesses. An activity in which we find pleasure and we perform well, can be called a strength. There can be a paradox situation in which we perform well in an activity without finding any pleasure. What will we call it? Woul we call it a strength or a weakness? If there is no pleasure, no matter how good you are, it's to be called a weakness. Anything that saps our energy, anything that does not get you to flow is to be called a weakness. Neurochemistry explains why. When we are positively engaged by a challenge, our brain is being soaked in a bath of substances triggered by the adrenal system. These chemicals prime the brain to stay attentive and interested, even fascinated, and energized for a

The Name of the Game

t. Intense motivation is, literally, an "adrenaline w that the amygdala houses the general brain undergirds motivation (Goleman, 1998). The ning that predisposes someone to take pleasure in one set of activities rather than another, as well as the repertoire of memory, feelings, and habits associated with those activities, is stored in the emotional memory banks of the amygdala and its related circuits. Our motives guide our awareness toward the opportunities they seek out. The amygdala is a kind of "neural doorway" through which whatever we care about – whatever motivates us – enters and is weighed in terms of its value as an incentive (J.D. Duffy, *The Neural Substrate of Emotions*, Psychiatric Annals, Jan. 1997). People who suffer brain diseases, trauma or a stroke that deprive them of their amygdala (leaving the rest of the brain intact) suffer from a disorder of motivation. They are unable to distinguish what matters most to them and what is irrelevant, between what moves them and what leaves them cold. The result is paralyzing apathy, or an indiscriminate, uncontrollable indulgence in appetites. The amygdala circuitry is what Goleman calls the low road. The instant response, what we can call "gut feeling". This motivational circuitry connects to the prefrontal lobes, the brain executive center (the high road), which brings a sense of context and appropriateness to the amygdala's surges. The prefrontal area houses an array of inhibitory neurons that can veto or tone down the amygdala's impulses, adding caution.

Goleman identifies four motivational variables that typify outstanding performers (D. Goleman, 2000, p.113) : ***Achievement drive, Commitment and initiative, and optimism.***

POTENTIAL WHAT FOR? AN INTEGRATED MODEL

Achievement drive: people with this competence are result oriented, with a high dive to meet their objectives and standards. They set for themselves and others challenging goals and *take calculated risk*. They pursue information to reduce uncertainty and find ways to do better. They *learn* how to improve their performance and they support enterprising innovations. The "calculated risk" variable and the "initiative" variable are two variables in which entrepreneurs rate particularly highly. It's on this particular variable we can see important cultural and values gap between organizations. McClelland found in his research that outstanding performers set more challenging goals for themselves; they often managed to enlarge the scope of their position by their initiatives. Their risk strategy is to set risky but manageable challenges. Entrepreneurial drive demands that people be comfortable taking risks but know how to calculate them carefully. This skill at taking smart risks is a mark of the successful entrepreneur. In the survey we carried out, what was striking was the reaction some HR Directors had when asked about entrepreneurial skills as a key-variable for assessing potential. In some cases reaction was positive, they perceived it as a very important trait that should be acknowledged and supported. In one case the HR Director related a current shift from a "good soldier" culture towards a more autonomy supportive and "entrepreneurial" culture. She said there was still a long way to go, but in terms of long-term strategy, businesses had to seriously consider this cultural change. She laughed saying *"good soldiers are rarely very creative, do you see what I mean?"*. In other cases the reaction was definitely negative, entrepreneurial traits were perceived as "risky", they were clearly not fitting with the company's culture. In one case "you have to do what is expected, possibly better than others" if you want to be noticed, in the other it's about "being committed, doing whatever it takes to maximize impact", using your courage, your entrepreneurial spirit and thinking in absolute terms, not in relative terms (i.e. being better than..., being smarter than...). Both approaches value performance, but while one is based on validation and values conformism, the other values commitment, initiative and autonomy. Optimism is key as we saw in the beginning of this chapter and the previous chapter when we discussed Albert Bendura's self-efficacy-theory, McClelland's achievement motivation theory and Edwin Lock and Gary Latham Goal-setting theory. If you are optimistic about your abilities, about your future achievements, if you are self-confident, studies show that you will handle challenges better, persist through difficulties and achieve better results (Martin Seligman and G. Buchanan studies of optimism and pessimism "Explanatory style", Hillsdale, NJ, 1995 and other studies cited in D.Goleman, *Working with Emotional Intelligence*, 2000, p.71).

Commitment and Initiative: The essence of commitment is making your goals and those of your organization one and the same. Commitment is emotional, it means we feel a strong attachment towards the organization we work for. Those who embrace an organization's mission are willing not just to make an important effort on its behalf, but to make sacrifices to meet a larger organizational goal. They find a sense of purpose in the larger mission, they are intrinsically motivated and use the organization's core values in making decisions and clarifying choices. They have initiative; they actively seek out opportunities and strategies to fulfill the group's mission. It's about an unselfish strategic vision, doing what's right in a long-term vision, in taking calculated risks and in sometimes taking decisions that are unpopular. The truly committed sometimes make unpopular decisions that are made to benefit the larger group in the medium-to-long term. For this to happen companies and organizations must have a well-formulated mission, employees need a clear sense of an organization's core values to feel committed. Those with initiative act without being compelled or forced by external pressures or events. They often anticipate needs and events, they take action to avoid problems before they are visible to anyone else. They think and plan ahead taking advantage of opportunities nobody else noticed, sometimes taking calculated risks; sometimes taking steps when nobody sees the need to and bending the rules when necessary to get the job done. This takes certain courage, entrepreneurial spirit, especially when others object. Those who tend to react to events, rather than anticipate and prepare for them, are those who lack initiative. Sometimes initiative means just very hard work, having perseverance, being proactive and sticking to it. Initiative needs self- and social awareness. Too much initiative, or in other terms the lack of self- and social awareness, can be dangerous. In order to avoid negative consequences, minding others is key.

Motives are a fundamental dimension, they are hard to change. You can however influence the focus and give a performance-focus or a more developmental and mastery-focus. Your organization can chose to have either a 'be good' or a 'get better' approach, depending upon circumstances, but also depending upon the values of the organization.

THE GROWTH DIMENSION

An old Chinese proverb says :

> *If you want one year of prosperity, grow grain;*
> *If you want ten years of prosperity, grow trees;*
> *If you want a hundred years of prosperity, grow people.*

Silzer and Church in their article *"the pearls and perils of identifying potential"* (in Industrial and Organizational Psychology 2, pp.377-412, 2009) identify three types of potential dimension:

1. A foundational dimension
2. A growth dimension
3. A career dimension

The foundational dimensions are the traits that are hard to change as we described above: in the first dimension Silzer and Church included *Cognitive abilities* and *Personality*. In the second, the growth dimension, they included *Learning* and *Motivation*. In the third, the career dimension, they included Leadership, Performance, Knowledge and Values. Of the three dimensions proposed by Silzer and Church I would retain just the first two :

- The foundational dimension
- The growth dimension.

POTENTIAL WHAT FOR? AN INTEGRATED MODEL

A career dimension presupposes experience and learning abilities. Learning in particular is a growth dimension and is, in a way, the gate-keeper of development (career means development within an organization if we want to use basic terms). If the motivation variables (that are part of the foundational dimension in our model) include:

- *Achievement drive,*

- *Commitment,*

- *Initiative and optimism,*

which are clearly linked to a career dimension, why would you need a third dimension? If the focus is on leadership skills and management skills, two variables that are key in most potential models, we can cast them also in a growth dimensions. This division in the dimension of potential suggests that both the foundational dimensions and the growth dimensions may be useful predictors of potential wide range of careers and talents pools, irrespective of their career path. There is one **sine-qua-non** condition that can be called a personality foundational pre-requisite, it's a foundational condition, not a fixed trait. We can call it a meta-cognitive ability, that will also determine how open the person is to feed-back, cognitive and emotional growth and learning: self-awareness. This is a competency that determines how we manage ourselves. Self-awareness means knowing one's internal states, preferences, resources and intuitions. How will a person be able to manage others, understand others, engage others, and lead others if he/she lacks this introspective ability? When hiring external talent or assessing internally, self-awareness should be a key-variable to be kept in mind. What are the terms used to describe himself/

herself, how she/he talks about motives, feelings and emotions, is aware of his/her values and goals and has structured arguments to link together those elements (recognizing and explaining in terms of what, why and how). This is the basis of all emotional competencies. Emotional competencies involve thought and skill. Golemand writes, "they involve some degree of skill in the realm of feelings, along with whatever other cognitive elements that are at play" (D. Goleman 2000, p.23). *Performance* on the other hand *is a consequence of these variables and traits*, not a condition.

Comparing the Potential Integrated Models. The first one below is the one proposed by Silzer & Church, which consists of three dimensions:

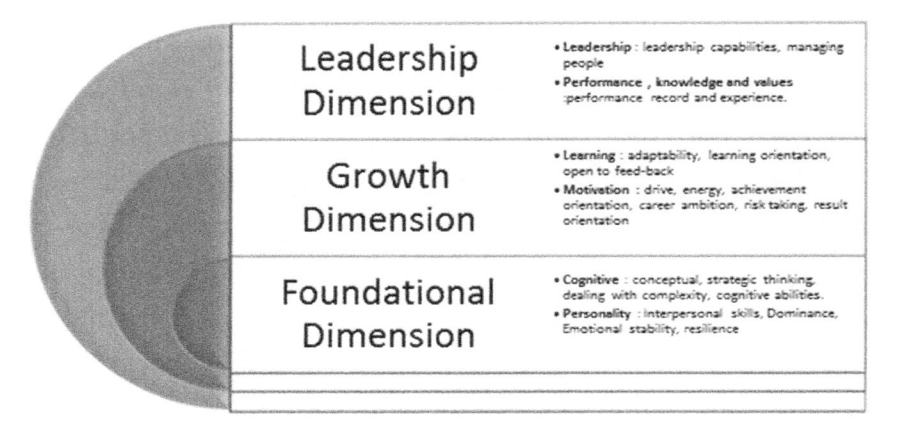

Leadership Dimension	• Leadership: leadership capabilities, managing people • Performance, knowledge and values: performance record and experience.
Growth Dimension	• Learning: adaptability, learning orientation, open to feed-back • Motivation: drive, energy, achievement orientation, career ambition, risk taking, result orientation
Foundational Dimension	• Cognitive: conceptual, strategic thinking, dealing with complexity, cognitive abilities. • Personality: interpersonal skills, Dominance, Emotional stability, resilience

Below is a comparison of Silzer & Church's model with a challenging integrated model that assumes as prerequisites: performance and a good level self-awareness. In this model we propose **motivation** and **Fluid Intelligence** as the foundational dimension, while personality and leadership skills are within the growth dimension (with no third career dimension):

POTENTIAL WHAT FOR? AN INTEGRATED MODEL

	SILZER AND CHURCH INTEGRATED POTENTIAL MODEL	PROPOSING A MODEL WITH DIFFERENT FOUNDATIONAL- & GROWTH DIMENSIONS Pre-conditions : performance and a good level of self-awareness
Foundational Dimensions	**Cognitive** : conceptual, strategic thinking, dealing with complexity, cognitive abilities. **Personality** : Interpersonal skills, Dominance, Emotional stability, resilience	**Cognitive abilities :** Fluid Intelligence G(f) ,working memory, certain 'learning agility' factprs, adaptability **Motivation:** achievement drive, energy, commitment, initiative (taking calculated risk), optimism.
Growth Dimensions	**Learning** : adaptability, learning orientation, open to feed-back **Motivation** : drive, energy, achievement orientation, career ambition, risk taking, result orientation	**Learning abilities presupposing a "growth mindset" and a "get-better" focus:** Crystallized intelligence and skill development **Personality :** Interpersonal skills, collaboration skills, self-regulation, EQ (See appendix 1) **Leadership skills :** lead engaging people, managing people, developing others, influencing, challenging status quo, taking calculated risk
Career Dimensions	**Leadership** : leadership capabilities, managing people **Performance , knowledge and values** :performance record and experience.	

The Name of the Game

If results have not been achieved, if performance is poor or average, something went wrong. Many interviewed HR Directors said that performance is something that can be perceived and assessed within a short period of time. You don't need four years to figure out if one of your employees is an average or an over-achiever. High achievers, those that exceed expectations, can be identified within less than a year, sometimes within less than six months. A pillar can also be a high-achiever. Having this in mind, I thought that performance is not a high potential dimension, it's a consequence of the other variables (motivation, personality traits, cognitive abilities etc.) and dimensions and is a prerequisite to being identified as having potential. A HR Director when asked if performance can be defined as a high-potential variable, replied that it was just a shortcut to identify top talent, a necessary but not a sufficient condition required to be in the key-talent pipeline or the high potential pool.

THE ULTIMATE SOURCES OF SATISFACTION

What are the ultimate sources of satisfaction? When over seven hundred people were asked this question at the age of retirement, at the end of a rewarding career, they answered that the most rewarding thing was the *creative challenge* and *stimulation of the work itself,* and the *chance to keep learning.* Much lower in the list came status, or pride, and even lower was financial gain. What organizations should think about is maintaining their employees, and in particular their top talent, in a constant 'learning mode'. Promotion is just part of the picture, to be promoted to a position that is not challenging does not mean much since the person won't learn, won't need to stretch. In this case it can be much more rewarding and stimulating to work on a challenging project without having a promotion. Of course it's better to have both, but if an organization has to choose, the second option is better if they want to keep high-potential talent (at least the ones that are not only "status focused"). There are companies that have high-potential lists and that communicate formally about who's on the list. They give financial incentives but are unable to retain their high-potentials. I interviewed a good number of "high-potential" employees who were looking for new opportunities because after spending 3-4 years in a position they weren't given visibility on the next steps and had the feeling of not learning anymore. They often said they learned during the first two years, during the third year they managed to enlarge as far as they could the scope of their position and at the end of the third year they felt they had seen all there was to see and learn ("on a fait le tour"). If the company does not give a promotion or a stretch assignment, there is no money in the world that will retain a top talent. Money is obviously important and should reward performance; it would be a mistake to reward potential. Potential is performance that isn't actual yet, the only way organizations can choose to reward potential, so that conceptually it makes sense and doesn't create a sense of injustice and inequity, is with long-term incentives. A remuneration that is not actual, that will take place in the

The Name of the Game

future. On the other hand there are exceptional employees that aren't particularly ambitious or have reached their incompetence edge, they are extremely trustworthy pillars, or they lack the motivation and drive to move up. They might have personal reasons, as is the case of Thomas who is a Senior IT manager, whose real passion is music and playing the piano. He wants an interesting and stimulating job, but still wants to have enough time to cultivate his passion. He does not have power motivation or great career ambition, nevertheless he is an excellent performer: a pillar. That's why annual interviews and talent reviews are so important. They are the occasion to give feedback on past performance, set the annual objectives, and last but not least, ask employees what they want, towards what they aspire and what their motives are, what moves them, what gives them pleasure. This is not to say that incentives don't matter, there is of course value in promotions, stock options and bonuses; however what really seems to matter is interest in the content, internal motives, passion, desire to stretch, to learn and develop one's skills. An interesting point that emerged in an interview with a HR Director about motivation is the difference he notices between men and women. McClelland affirmed that achievement motivation theory is intended more for male than for females. The result has been that when females have been studied, the results often have not been the same as those found in males; in fact frequently there have been no results at all, where results might have been expected. McClelland assumes that females have higher fear of success than males, which would lower their achievement motivation scores. According to the perception and observations of this HR Director, women are not explicit, they don't make it as clear as men what they want, it's not about achievement or motivation scores. He assumes that they sometimes have very high achievement motivation, but expect to be noticed and gratified, expect external acknowledgment of their merits. This makes it more difficult to know what they really aspire to. It's another behavioral pattern, but that doesn't mean they have less achievement motivation, less drive or less ambition. It's about analyzing and creating new references of behavioral patterns, a new approach and new scales to measure women achievement motivation, since the one developed and applied to men does not seem to work when considering women. McKinsey & Company, in the last Quarterly Review (May 2012) presented a study titled "*Unlocking the full potential of women at work*" (Joanna Barsh and Lareina Yee). Based on an in-depth investigation on 60 leading companies, their research reveals that many organizations are closer to unlocking the full potential of women at work, meaning that women are advancing beyond middle management positions. The article points out that top-management must be hands-on and visibly committed to achieving the gender-diversity goal and that HR leaders believe that gender diversity is a business imperative. What great looks like? Based on the figures from the top third of participants, they set the metric at having at least 22 percent female representation on the executive committee; 19 companies (out of 60 companies) met this bar. They set the bar at 22 percent probably because figures were not so encouraging and we don't want to know how

The Name of the Game

many companies have over 30 percent of women at executive committee level. They write that what has been described as "stubborn barriers", are structural obstacles, lifestyle choices, institutional mind-sets and individual mind-sets. Leadership teams have been working hard at removing them, addressing the lack of sponsorship, limited flexibility and unconscious biases. The question that should be posed is: who composes the leadership teams? Who are those that define the rules of the game? If the leadership team that defines the rules of the game is composed mainly of men – or of those women that learned to act like men in order to advance - it will be difficult to avoid these "stubborn barriers". In this article the authors discuss the 'institutional mind-sets', meaning that "used to successful executives being –acting like- men, leaders expect women to model the same behavior.". The article's conclusion focuses on examples of "Women who are making it work" and the traits that enabled them to step up to senior executive roles: Robust work ethic (going beyond what is asked of them), results orientation (relentless focus on performance), resilience (persevere in times of adversity), persistence in getting feedback (looking for feedback) and team leadership (encouraging people to stretch and grow). The traits are always the same ones; they apply to men as well as to women. However what remains fuzzy is _who_ gives the feedback – if it's always men who give the feed-back according to the same rules and a leadership model inspired by male's behavior, it does not mean that women make it to the top because barriers were abolished, but simply because they behave according to a male's leadership model. This is the real challenge that lies ahead. One of the interviewed HR Directors explained that this is a fundamental issue when identifying and selecting potential, women tend to be excluded because the leadership models have been developed from a male behavioral standpoint. In his organization they are now developing a female-oriented leadership model that will help to better assess women's leadership potential.

Chapter 5

POTENTIAL IN DIFFERENT GAMES: A COMPARATIVE STUDY

RESEARCH DESIGN AND METHODOLOGY

The previous four chapters are the theoretical foundation of this research. The intention was to provide a lens for decoding and interpreting in a critical way the coming section.

The primary aim of this chapter is to present the research design which has been selected to answer the research question. This chapter starts with a discussion of the research methodology, followed by a discussion of research philosophy and associated approach. In the following section the research strategy and the research process will be presented. The chapter will then conclude with a discussion of the importance of this theme in the medium- and long-term, considering the ethical issues involved, that should be a concern for organizations and for the values they want to embody.

RESEARCH METHODOLOGY

The major aim of this research is to provide a comparative study of policies and practices that concern key-talent within organizations and define how and when high-potentials should be assessed. First the focus will be set on what organizations put behind the term high-potential. Then there will be a comparative analysis of talent management practices and policies concerning how different organizations handle their high-potentials. The aim is to describe and discuss <u>what</u> they do when they evaluate, try to motivate and retain their top talent, as well as comparing and discussing <u>how</u> they do it.

Thus, different methodologies and approaches have been considered at the beginning. A suggestion was to study what is done by the assessment centers in terms of potential identification and evaluation. However, this approach would have described the present situation without any additional value. Moreover, assessment centers are very expensive and research shows that they convey only 14% of trustworthy data concerning *potential* assessment. Besides, this field study showed that very few organizations use assessment centers, and among these very few some use them as developmental tool- rather than an assessing tool. There will be a section dedicated to this topic, but a marginal one if compared to the rest. Another approach that was considered, but not retained, was to submit to HR executives a questionnaire. In this case the idea was to collect a large amount of data that would help lead to a quantitative analysis. It would have been a statistical approach. A semi-structured interview guide is the approach that has been retained. The aim was to gather qualitative rather than quantitative data and possibly, given it was semi-structured, to gain some interesting insights and leave the interviewee more at ease to develop and explain specific aspects if needed. The interview guide is made up of 25 questions. Fifteen are what can be called the 'core-questions', the supplementary ten permitted entering into detail, if necessary. There are three types of questions in the interview guide:

- questions focusing on policies, meaning the official standpoint of the organizations about a specific topic (as for example to have or not to have high-potential lists);

- questions focusing on practices (this part is particularly interesting since the questions aim at disclosing what lies beneath policies. Meaning that we come across grey-areas and very interesting details that are more or less consistent with official positions);

- questions focusing on the personal standpoint of the interviewee, his personal position and his/her feeling about a given policy and/or practice. (See complete interview guide in the Appendix 1)

RESEARCH PHILOSOPHY AND INSPIRATION

The philosophical framework for this research is non-cartesian. The writings of David Hume in particular, have been inspirational and represent in a certain way the background, the philosophical framework of this research. The aim is to understand, accepting the limits of the exercise.

The non-linear systems described in the previous chapter are inscribed in this tradition. Hume's *empiricism* is defined by his treatment of the science of human nature as an empirical inquiry, rooted in *experience and observation*, to his limitation of investigation to "original principles," and his repudiation of any attempt to discover "*ultimate original qualities*" in the study of human nature. One of the aspects of Hume's *skepticism* is about the possibility of metaphysical theories, or any "hypothesis or system" that attempts to go beyond experience and observation. When discussing non-linear systems, I had Hume's empistemology in mind, the so-called *Problem of Induction*. This may be the area of Hume's thought where his skepticism about human powers of reason is most pronounced. The problem concerns the explanation of how we are able to make inductive inferences. Hume's solution to this problem is to argue that, rather than reason, natural instinct explains this human ability. He asserts that *"Nature, by an absolute and uncontournable necessity has determined us to judge as well as to breathe and feel"*.

Concerning human behaviour, Hume's position is that human behaviour is governed by "custom", by habits rather than by reason. In a famous sentence in the *Treatise*, Hume circumscribes reason's role in the production of action: "*Reason is, and ought only to be the slave of the passions, and can never pretend to any other office than to serve and obey them*". If the assumption was that reason governs human behaviour there wouldn't be much hope concerning the possibility of improvement. If it's beliefs, custom and habits that govern our way of thinking and acting, as implicit beliefs do, then there is a good margin for improvement ahead and we can make an effort to change. Changing one's beliefs, customs and habits is not an easy task, nevertheless it remains in the domain of the 'possible' endeavors. Desires and passions and our emotions move us. D. Goleman's emotional intelligence theory is inscribed in this philosophical tradition. EQ plays a central role in all our actions, behaviors, achievements and understanding of human nature.

RESEARCH PROCESS

Before starting the research interviews, four pilot interviews were carried out to test the interview guideline and timings. The first pilot interview was carried out with a friend who is HR Director of a division within a large listed company. He helped in defining the order of the questions and going deeper into certain details. The second pilot interview was with another acquaintance, who is HR manager in an organization where the talent management policies and practices do not correspond to her values. There is a growing gap between what she perceives as just and equitable and what is applied as a norm in her company. Her position and arguments showed that it was interesting to check by adding a few questions in the interview guide, whether the practices and policies of the company corresponded to and were consistent with the personal standpoint and values of the interviewed person. The third and fourth interviews were useful for determining the question order, so that depending on the answers the interview would maintain a consistent structure and timing. Each pilot interview took about one hour, which helped to organize the interviews.

Fifteen Senior HR Directors were interviewed between February 9th 2012 and June 16th 2012. Most of the interviews were conducted by phone, because of time constraints. A few (about a quarter) were conducted face to face and in both circumstances it was agreed that I would take notes. Group HR Directors, Heads of Global Executive Talent, Group Heads of Learning and Development and Regional HR Directors from European and American multinationals were interviewed. It could be said that interviewing only fifteen people cannot yield meaningful results. However, HR Directors in each organization and country face similar circumstances, options, questions and challenges, which allow the identification of patterns. A shared conception of high-potential is a person that will occupy a leadership position in the future. The notion of what is a leader, however, can vary depending on the organization's culture. Maxwell defined a leader as "one who knows the way, goes the way, and shows the way" (cited Kleiner et al. 2005, p.54). A couple of thousand years earlier Lao Tzu defined the highest type of leader in those terms :

> *The highest type of leader is one of whose existence the people are barely aware.*
> *Next comes one whom they love and praise.*
> *Next comes one whom they fear.*

Next comes one whom they despise and defy.
When you are lacking faith,
Others will be unfaithful to you.

The sage is self-effacing and scanty of words.
When his task is accomplished and things have been completed,
All the people say, "We ourselves have achieved it!"

DATA ANALYSIS

Qualitative data are complex, due to the fact that they are difficult to standardize. A challenge was to create a positive and developmental atmosphere with the interviewees, in order to foster good communication and mutual trust. It was agreed that there would be a no-name policy, complete confidentiality concerning the name of the companies and of the interviewed HR professionals. This was also important to ensure that data was reliable and trustworthy. In order to achieve this positive and trusting atmosphere the interview guide was always presented as "work in progress". The 25 questions were clearly formulated, but interviewees were ask to comment on questions, to make remarks and volunteer criticism if they felt it would enrich the exercise and improve the quality of data. The interview became often a rich discussion and exchange, this enabled to go more in depth into a specific subjects. At the end of the interview feed-back was always sought. Interviews were conducted in English, French and Italian.

FIELD STUDY RESULTS AND FINDINGS

The chapter outlines the findings of the semi-structured interviews with senior HR executives. From a total of sixteen cases, all expressed interest in the subject and most said that some of the policies were currently under discussion at executive committee level concerning how to best manage the high-potential pool. Interviewee's names were altered, in order to assure anonymity. In addition, company names have been withheld and have been assigned letters (Company A, Company B..).

This chapter is structured into three main themes. The first section discusses interviewee's definitions and feelings about high-potential programs. Next came findings concerning how they manage talent in general, versus high-potential employees, comparing policies and approaches and focusing on the different dimensions they selected for assessing talent. The third section will address the theme of personal reflections and personal values.

MEANING OF "HIGH-POTENTIAL" AND FEELINGS ABOUT THIS SUBJECT

Before asking for definitions, the subject was introduced by a general question: do you have a high-potential list within your organization? Compared to the Silzer and Church article where they found 100% of organizations having a high-potential program, our research shows that the majority do have lists, however a few don't. Those that don't have high-potentials lists, chose to avoid this approach to talent, because they judged it to be an "elitist" approach. Moreover, among those organizations who do have high-potential lists the approach to this population can be dramatically different. An interesting aspect that emerged, concerns subtle linguistic differences that are nevertheless of the utmost importance. Some call them high-potentials, others decided to avoid this term because it would imply that there are "average" or "low" potentials, which would be perceived as non-equitable. Thus, they coined other terms : **"Best bets"**, **"Next talent generation"**, **"CTG population"** (Capacity To Grow Population), **"Evolving key-talent"** (EKT lists), simply **"Talents"** or **"Rising Talents pipeline"**. We could say, at a first glance, that all those organizations that employ "lists" have a very similar approach to talent management. That would be a mistake. More than half of the organizations decided to avoid the term "high-potential" for example, which is a relevant point to be put forward. Several HR Directors had been discussing how to manage this promising population during the past few executive committees and were still not clear about the approach they wanted to adopt (meaning that discussions at group level are ongoing and tough). Just looking at the terms they decided to employ for those talented individuals, we can notice the differences in approach. Compared to the term "high-potential" which is a label that seems to be a fixed trait that won't be changing in time or depending on circumstances, the terms mentioned above that are meant to replace the term "high-potential" imply something

The Name of the Game

more flexible and open. "Best bets" as "Capacity to grow" as well as "Rising talents" or "Evolving key-talent", implies the fact that their future is not set in stone one and for all. They contain the notion of probability: their future depends on many variables that cannot be carved in stone at a given moment in time. A Global Executive Talent Development Director made an interesting point about the High-Potential population she managed. She made it clear at the very beginning when asked about the existence of high-potential lists, that High-potential is not a state, it's not independent of time, place, context and purpose. She said "it's an appreciation, a judgment made at a certain moment in time and it can change. It's not a contract". This is the way she communicated to high-potentials they had been identified. Furthermore she specified the fact that they were "high-potentials" for a given future position, it was always in a succession planning context. In this case 'high-potential' isn't a label, it's a possibility to step up towards a given position. It answers to the question : potential *what for*? I asked her what her personal point of view was and her answer was striking, since she perceived the need to change the model, to change the variables that lay behind the term high-potential:

"What is key in my point of view is that leaders don't need to be motivated by labels, they motivate themselves. They have a vision. If I think about high-potentials in my organization, I think of good and competent officers. They do what they are asked to do and according to expectations. Perhaps it's all companies need and want. However, I personally think that companies if they want to be competitive in the 21st century should give a chance to creativity and team effort, rather than praising single individuals when they do what's expected. For that

you don't need officers, good soldiers, your rather need co-entrepreneurs. I am referring to those who don't need external stimuli in order to perform, those who are autonomous, those who have initiative, critical thinking. Those who take risks for the sake of higher performance in the future and are able to engage themselves and others for a common objective and purpose".

She was the first interviewee, her critical approach showed that things were not simple. At least not as simple and "crystal clear" as many articles on this topic seemed to suggest. The results reported by Silzer & Church about hundred percent high-potential programs in major listed organizations, as the recent article by C.Fernandez-Araoz, B.Groysberg and N.Nohria, "*How to Hang on to your High-potentials*" (HBR, October 2011) tend to over-simplify the topic. Arraoz and al. also interviewed 70 companies all around the world that have high-potential programs. They only speak of "high-potential programs", omnipresent programs, they cite best practices like GE, Unilever, PepsyCo and Shell (among others) omitting the information that some of those best practices decided not to use the term "high-potential" and have very different approaches to talent management and to what can be called a "program". After this first interview, for the first time I thought about the notion of a "successful program". It made me realize that "High-potentials" don't look the same everywhere, what organizations put behind the term 'high-potential' often depends upon the company's culture, values and needs. That is to say that what appears to be a detail, a minor difference in the term the organization decided to use, does count. Moreover, various organizations reported having more than one category of top talent. There are companies that report having a generic "high-potential" category, most of the time referring to younger talent that is observed during a given period of time; there are other companies that are clearly against this kind of "generic" high-potential label and employ the term high-potential only in a "succession-planning"-context. In this case a high-potential is always referred to in relation to a *target job*. Given the fact that this "high-potential approach" is very specific, since it necessarily refers to a specific position (next step position) these organizations don't hesitate to tell high-potentials explicitly about their options for the next move (transparency policy).

Twenty percent of the organizations approached don't have High-Potential Programs. They <u>decided</u> not to have an "elitist" approach to talent. It's a choice, the result of a debate, not a lack of talent management strategy. They are contingency focused; they have a succession planning approach to talent. The other 80% have high-potential lists, however less than 50% employ the term High-Potentials. To be precise, 40% chose the term "High-potentials", the other 60% decided to avoid the use of this term and use other terms instead. They avoided a "caste" culture, preferring a "talent" approach.

HP versus Non-HP cultures

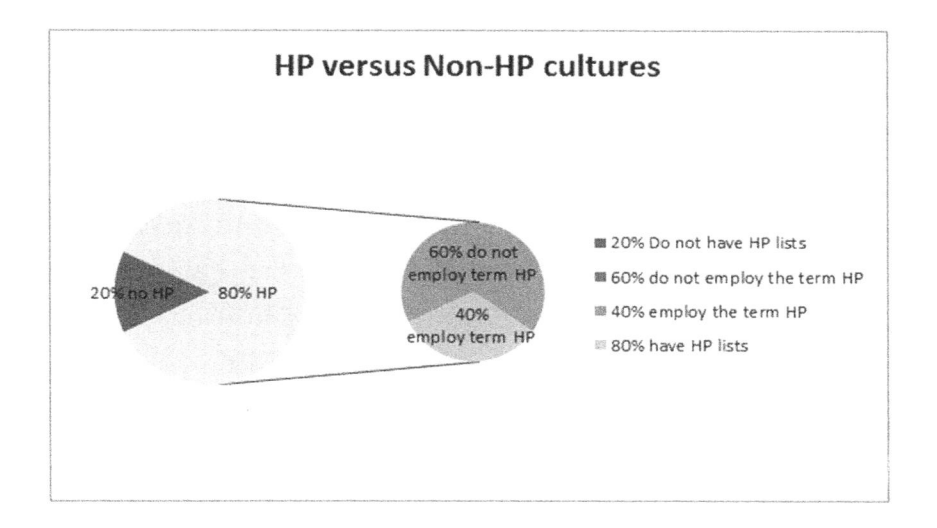

- 20% Do not have HP lists
- 60% do not employ the term HP
- 40% employ the term HP
- 80% have HP lists

20% no HP / 80% HP
60% do not employ term HP / 40% employ term HP

DEFINITIONS : THE WHAT AND THE HOW OF POTENTIAL

Definitions may vary, but they are substantially similar when it comes to defining potential. *Potential* is defined as *the capacity to move up 1 or 2 levels within a time span of 1 to 5 years*. Every organization has its own rules concerning the time span. *Most say one level up in 1 to 3 years, and two levels up in 3 to 5 years*. The meaning of one or more levels up is not only hierarchical, it can also refer to :

- International mobility
- Access to a larger scope of responsibility
- A functional career evolution
- Transversal mobility towards a position with greater responsibilities/ Project Mgmt

The Name of the Game

Performance is defined as the extent to which objectives where achieved. Performance is the "entry ticket" as an HR Executive explained. It's the necessary condition to be eligible. 100% of the organizations reported that performance is a necessary but not sole prerequisite to being identified, and to be selected if there is a list. Performance in a certain way is a "given". Every organization has a set of conditions that should be met in addition to performance. These conditions, the so called "key-competencies" and "traits" that lie behind the term "high-potential", "key-talent", "capacity to grow individuals", or "best bets" are in some cases similar and sometimes very different, as will be discussed in the next section. Furthermore, some organizations had various categories of "High-potentials" or "key-talent". Most of those categories included leadership skills as a necessary competency; however a few companies reported having an "expert" high-potential pool. For example, depending on experience and performance, one organization reported having one category for young promising talent. Those few are identified during the first years of their career within the organization and are those who can step up 2-3 levels in a short period of time. The second category, called the "best bets", are those that the organization has identified for precise positions (succession planning at executive level). Within the "best bets" category they have different populations that are considered, according to their "diversity policy": women (called Rising Talents) or for other populations "diversity best bets", making sure all categories are well represented. The fact of having different categories of key-talent, or just different talent pools seems to be interesting. Experience apparently shows, as a senior Group Head of Talent sustained that:

"It's not the young over-achievers and over-performers that went up higher in the organization. It's not the first in class that stepped up higher, rather those who had vision, who were able to engage and motivate others. I would say those that almost ascended despite themselves. Those that were ambitious in terms of learning rather than desperate for career advancement (ambitieux de gravir les échelons)".

The Performance dimension includes achievement and results orientation, which is the WHAT that makes up performance. Moreover, most organizations integrated, some only recently, also an Emotional Intelligence dimension, that can be defined as the HOW.

More than half of the approached organizations decided not to use the 9-box grid, where performance is matched against potential. The 9-box matrix, as discussed in the first chapter, is a strange exercise not only in terms of inductive reasoning, but because both of the variables are all but evident and easy to measure. Besides the fact, that it depends upon the person who is performing the evaluation, which is an additional variable that should be taken into account.

The Name of the Game

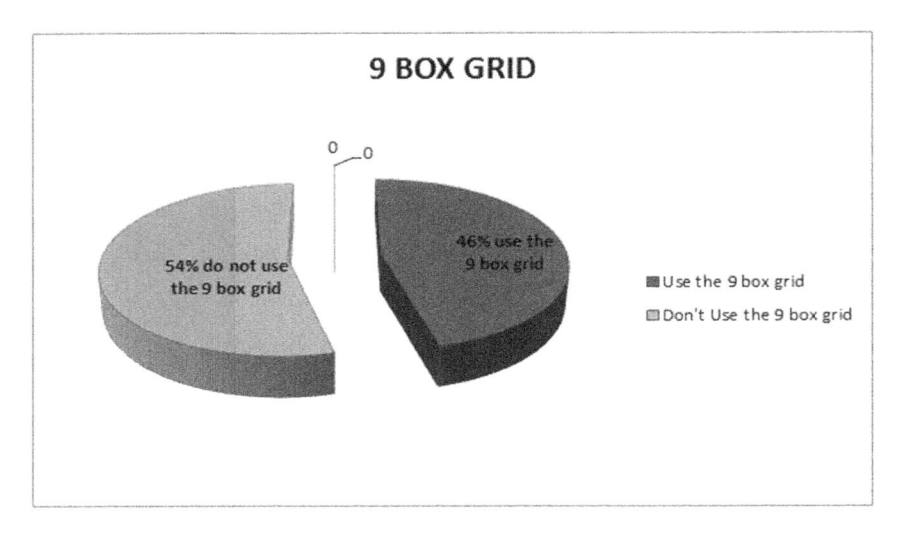

9 BOX GRID

- 46% use the 9 box grid
- 54% do not use the 9 box grid

The HR Training and Development Director of a large corporation within the Financial Services Sector said that at Group level they had decided not to employ this tool, whereas they gave almost complete freedom of choice to divisions concerning all possible assessment and development tools (assessment-center, coaching, training etc.). Another HR Director from the Pharmaceutical Sector on the other hand introduced the 9 box grid this year. She made an interesting point saying *"We started using the 9 box grid this year. It was a choice made at Group level. It assumes we speak about absolute values, while I think it is restrictive since the position does grow or not depending on whom is occupying it. I am personally against this tool, since it's not dynamic and does not take into account evolution. It just helps with visualizing and linking talent to performance (among peers), since potential is a very fuzzy concept to put on a graph and cannot be generically employed"*. In a certain way the 9 box grid gives a snapshot, a point in time, something that is crystalized but useful for decision-making. An example that was given was an externally hired HR Director who steps in and needs to have a general overview of the talent pipeline at a glance. Nevertheless, it lacks plasticity, context and dynamics, and the fact of seeing people in boxes has a limited absolute value. Three other large organizations use the 9 box grid. One of those organizations, in the energy sector, uses it as one of the main tools of their Talent Management practice. They have a top-down approach; they assess on the job, take references and do annual appraisal interviews that prepare for the annual people (or talent) review. The 9 box grid is the main aid-tool to assessment, since it is during the annual people review that people's performance is discussed between operational managers and HR managers and people are put into "boxes".

The Name of the Game

This annual talent review is an open discussion, it is key because it's a way to limit subjectivity and expose different perceptions in what can be described as a "multiple perception" exercise that leads to a more objective appreciation of each individual. Then every individual's performance and potential is benchmarked against his/her peers. Since the 9 box grid was integrated into the group IT system a couple of years ago, it nevertheless became quite controversial. Many things have changed since then. The company has decided on a non-transparency policy, they decided not to tell high-potentials they are on the list for the following reasons (we will return to this subject later): equity reasons, to avoid creating expectations and to avoid arrogance and elitist feelings among those that have been selected. The controversy is that they cannot keep this information confidential now that it is in their IT system, once it has been published somewhere people have the right (legal right) to access it, if they wish to. "*Most don't ask*", said the HR Director, "*nevertheless we don't always feel at ease because some people want to know which box they were put into. This isn't always easy to handle and we are obliged to tell them. Before this tool became an applied IT program, things were different. I would say that our Group was much more development-oriented. This might be a consequence of the economic crisis we are getting through*". The organization still uses development tools and programs; however what was interesting in her account was that the choice of tools can make behaviours and values shift. An interesting aspect she reported about the use of this tool, is that surprisingly HR managers are those who are most interested to know which box they were put into and pushed to get the information about whether or not they were on the high-potential list. This reveals that there are consequences to certain decisions, if people want to know their label to feel reassured or frustrated, it means that the organization is creating a fixed-mindset environment and employees are slipping into it. That is probably what the HR Director meant by saying that before this tool was integrated into the system at group level, she perceived a much more "developmental" environment and approach to talent. There are many positive points nevertheless that are worth mentioning: the joint effort and open discussion of HR executives and operational managers during the people review, the effort meant to get as close as possible to an objective result and the fact that the final word within this organization is left to the HR professionals that gather all the information and are, in a sense, the gate keepers.

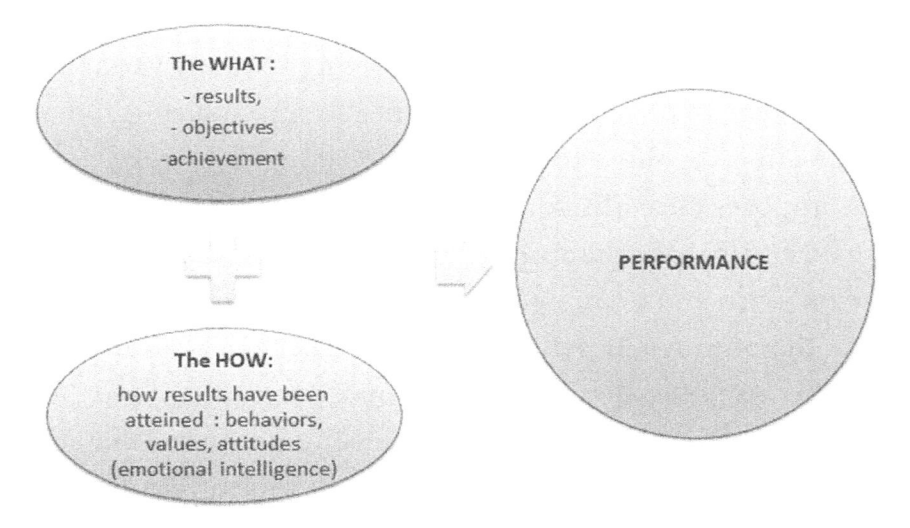

The WHAT:
- results,
- objectives
- achievement

+

The HOW:
how results have been atteined : behaviors, values, attitudes (emotional intelligence)

PERFORMANCE

Most of the organizations, some to a greater degree and others to a lesser degree, assess performance on results and achievements as well as on behavioural aspects, values and attitudes. Trying to answer the question: how did this

The Name of the Game

manager hold his position? Was he/she open? Sharing information? Delegating and trusting the team? Engaging others? Challenging the status quo and consensus? These few examples of what lies behind the evaluation of performance, in particular when focused on potential and how results have been achieved. A solid performer can achieve and over-achieve in terms of results, but he/she can lack self- assurance to challenge status quo and consensus for example. A future leader cannot lack this attitude. Behaviours, attitudes and values are necessary if we are to assess potential. The variables are so numerous that at the end of the exercise, all we can make is a "bet". The choice of this term, for a high-potential population, shows a humble attitude, consciousness of the limits of inference and acknowledging the limits of human judgment capabilities when applied to the future. When facing so many variables, in a system that we tend to simplify to a reassuring linear cause-effect reality, the fact of speaking of "best bets" presupposes clear thinking and acceptance of limits. There are no crystal balls that predict the future, we can go through the exercise and increase the chances of making a good bet, sometimes even a 'best bet'. Time is the necessary additional variable to prove them, this is beyond our control. Further boxes that need to be ticked in assessing potential that are often cited: strategic vision, drive, optimism, leadership skills (among others). Interestingly, the 9 box matrix was adjusted by an organization crossing achievements with values & behaviours. This HR professional, who is Head of Group Talent in the Services Sector, reported using a matrix that has PERFORMANCE on the Y-axis and "VALUES, BEHAVIOURS & ATTITUDES" on the X-axis, instead of "generic" Potential. This matrix helps visualize hard skills crossed with soft skills : those in the F, H and I box are those that are identified as the A-players because results are matched with great people-skills (emotional intelligence).

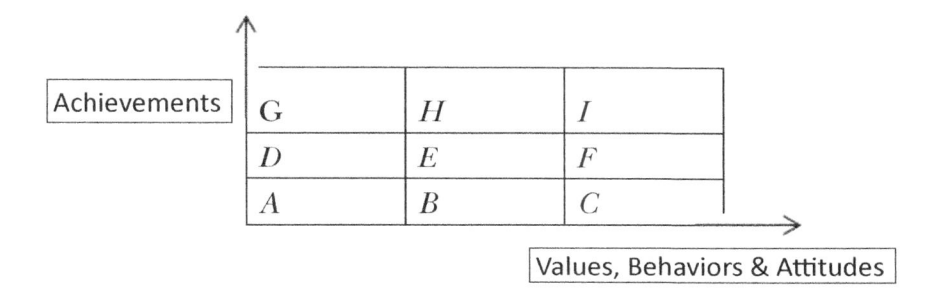

Achievements

G	H	I
D	E	F
A	B	C

Values, Behaviors & Attitudes

Let's look at an overview of the criteria that are taken into account when assessing potential besides of course achievements. Below is a comparison between two models, one from the services sector and the second one from the industry sector. The choice of comparing these two models instead of others is explained and justified below.

The Name of the Game

COMPANY X : What are the key-values, attitudes and behaviors?

Courage : takes calculated risk, challenge status quo and consensus.

Clear thinkers: embraces ambiguity and uncertainty, is adaptive; connects strategy to purpose in a way that inspires; takes decisions using knowledge, experience, network and instinct (analytical, decisive, considers alternatives, communication, deals with ambiguity, agile learner).

Inclusiveness : welcomes opposing thoughts and ideas, listens and remains humble; works collaboratively, respects individuals and cultures, drives engagement and commitment.

Imagination/innovation (creativity) : generates innovative ideas and makes it happen; encourages risk taking and learns from success/failure; challenges bureaucracy and non-value-added work, drives speed and simplicity

Customer Focus : Defines success through the customer's eyes
(scale of measurement : low, medium, acceptable, good, outstanding)

Leadership skills :

Integrity and credo-based actions (builds trust, tells truth, demonstrates genuine caring for people)

Strategic thinking (driven to envision a better future, takes any role or job and makes it better, a change agent)

Big picture orientation with attention to details (able to operate in two "worlds" simultaneously, sees the why as well as the what and can zoom in or out as needed

Ability to inspire and motivate: motivates and empowers others to achieve a desired action, enjoys developing a diverse group of people, instills confidence, brings out the best in others, invests time to be personally "connected"

Intellectual curiosity : sees the possibilities, willing to experiment

Collaboration and Teaming : puts interest of enterprise above own, works well across functions and groups, builds team effectively, instills a global mindset.

Sense of urgency : proactively senses and responds to problems and opportunities or shed non-viable business

Self-awareness and adaptability : resilient, has personal modesty and humility, willing to learn from others, patient, optimistic, flexible and adaptable

POTENTIAL IN DIFFERENT GAMES

COMPANY Y: What are the key-values, attitudes and behaviors?

Assumption N°1 : Potential can change over time

Assumption N° 2 – *Future state of performance should be given attention instead of focusing solely on "promotability"*.

Conditions sine-qua-non :

current outstanding performance, skills and motivation to move up, capabilities to learn and meet the competencies/skills required at a higher level in the future.

Values :

Customer focus : we listen to our customers, understand their needs and propose customized solutions and services…

Developing people : we value and maintain a permanent dynamics of *professional development for everyone*, fostering a *feed-back culture.*

Innovating, deciding and acting with agility: Courage and passion are essential. To achieve growth we encourage calculated risk taking, action-oriented employees…

Performing through teaming : 1+1= >2 , meaning that we are more efficient collectively, we encourage diversity as a way to enrich teams.

Key-behaviours :

Curiosity : See the possibilities (identify challenges and opportunities; willing to experiment (seek opportunities to learn and grow professionally); cultivates new ideas (supports others to think with an open mind-set), comfortable with ambiguity and uncertainty (makes progress and remains focused under ambiguous and complex situations)

Self-Awareness and learning agility/adaptability: *Actively seeks feed-back*; knows their strength and weaknesses, appreciates constructive criticism, *bounces back quickly from disappointment and mistakes*; learns and moves on quickly; Asserts personal ideas and opinions, using productive influence; demonstrates awareness of how his/her actions or interactions impact others.

Cooperation and Team spirit: is superior at building collaboration and teamwork across the local and global organization,; works to help others build strong, productive relationships across the organization; rewards direct reports and others for cultivating a strong business relationships with people from other areas of the organization; works to identify and ensure best practices and innovations are used on a local basis; *demonstrates ability to lead teams through change or transformation*.

Prudent risk taking : inner confidence to take risks and learn from experience; demonstrates the courage to stand alone on ideas and opinions; makes it safe for others to try new ideas and take appropriate risks; *treats mistakes as learning experience;* challenges the status quo, to identify ways of doing things better and faster. Takes risk in order to drive innovation, encouraging others to achieve innovative results.

Strategic thinking: driven to envision a better future – thinks strategically to create growth; makes complex issues easy for others to understand; translates vision and strategy into actionable goals and priorities; is a change agent.

The decision to compare the values and key-behaviours of these two organizations (and not others) was taken for the following reasons:

- It wouldn't be possible to compare in detail 15 different models;

- Comparison was decided upon the two most detailed models we had at our disposal;

- The values and key-behaviours required for identification and selection of top-talent are very similar across organizations, what changes is how they are structured (which has marginal relevance)

- These two displayed models enable us, due to their apparent similarity, to discuss what makes the difference, as apparently little details do.

- Realize that what makes the difference, what is really relevant, is not the "what", but rather the **HOW**: meaning how these policies are **applied**.

THE GREY-AREAS: HOW POLICIES ARE APPLIED

The interesting part of the exercise is not to compare two very different models and to show that one is better than another, because of particular values and behaviours that are quoted in one organization, while they are ignored in the other. Everybody has access to D. Goleman's (among others) research and publications and can elaborate a

POTENTIAL IN DIFFERENT GAMES

set of key-attitudes, behaviours and values (i.e. Working with Emotional Intelligence) to identify and assess their high-potential population. What makes this comparative exercise interesting are "subtle linguistic differences", the fact that some aspects are repeatedly underlined and last but not least, as mentioned above, <u>how</u> they are applied. A talent model that makes sense in a given organization due to business needs, environment, context, values, won't work nor make sense in another organization. Nevertheless there are some interesting assumptions that can make the difference. Regarding how attitudes, behaviours and values are applied, first of all, if we consider the first assumption (Company Y) that states that **Potential can change over time,** it means that there is not a particular time in terms of age, or in terms of career stage or seniority that should be retained as "the best moment" to assess potential. It implies that it's an *on-going process*. Moreover it implies that talent is not limited to the same pool of "usual suspects" that are assessed over and over again, year after year, (except of course the new hires). It presupposes that there is a chance that can be due to context, timing, interest, competencies, passion, experience, behaviour and many others possible variables that someone that is not on the HP list becomes a star.

This does not mean that COMPANY X does not apply this principle, but it's not a clearly stated assumption.

The Name of the Game

- "Potential can **change** over time"
- identification and selection is an **ongoing** process
- the organization is not fishing among the "**usual suspects**" over and over again

The second assumption (Company Y) is that future state of performance should be given attention instead of focusing solely on "promotability". This is a clear critical approach to the definition of High-Potential itself. As mentioned at the beginning of this chapter, the definition of potential is a matter of "promotability", meaning that a high-potential will step up one level in 1-3 years and/or up two levels in a time span of 3-5 years on average (some organizations have shorter time spans for two upward moves, i.e. 2-4 years; others prefer not to give time ranges and leave it fuzzy). In a certain way those that prefer to keep it fuzzy are conscious that they might fall into the trap they built. They are afraid of creating too many expectations about promotion within a given time span, since most of the time the promotion options are not clear two to three years in advance. The needs of the company in terms of where to put resources in four-five years is not an evident exercise, our institutions are struggling to keep up with major political, economic, technological, and social change. All those factors are driving profound transformation of our organizational models, making "predictability and stability elusive, if not impossible" (R.Boyatzis, A.McKee 2005). In this case, the "keep it fuzzy" policy is not a bad choice; it has the advantage of pointing straight to the problem and limits of the exercise. Promotion is a label, a validation process that makes somebody step up in the hierarchy. The company that shifts the focus from "promotability" (access to a new label/validation), to future "performance"(in term of new acquired competencies), is an organization that sets the focus on development. What do they mean by focusing on the "future state of performance" instead of just "promotability"? It means doing whatever is necessary to sustain learning and development in a feed-back rich environment in the long term, a sustained effort over time.

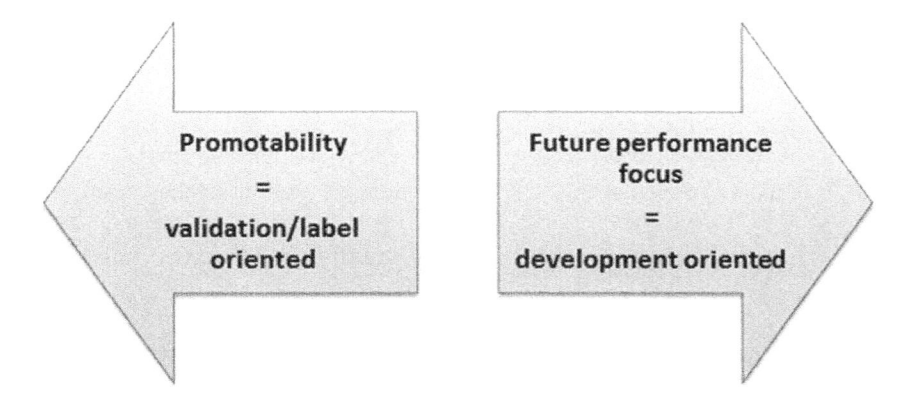

Promotability = validation/label oriented

Future performance focus = development oriented

That's why some organizations decided to avoid giving clear time spans or focussing on "career milestones". What matters is to observing who does and who doesn't learn from mistakes, who is open to feed-back, who is agile in learning and in adapting. In order to change from a validation culture to a developmental culture, these details must be kept in mind: subtle linguistic choices count. Where to start from? A good starting point is to observe how people, in particular those that are on the high-potential list, react to setback.

The Name of the Game

In both companies, X and Y, we have a strong feedback culture. Feedback cultures help develop self-awareness, help us to know better our own strengths and weaknesses and to learn from mistakes. However, feedback can be very different in its nature. As we saw in the previous chapters discussing Dweck's theory, a feedback session can be a sort of 'judgment', it can be a generic praise or a generic criticism that tends to label people; or, on the other hand, it can be specific and growth oriented.

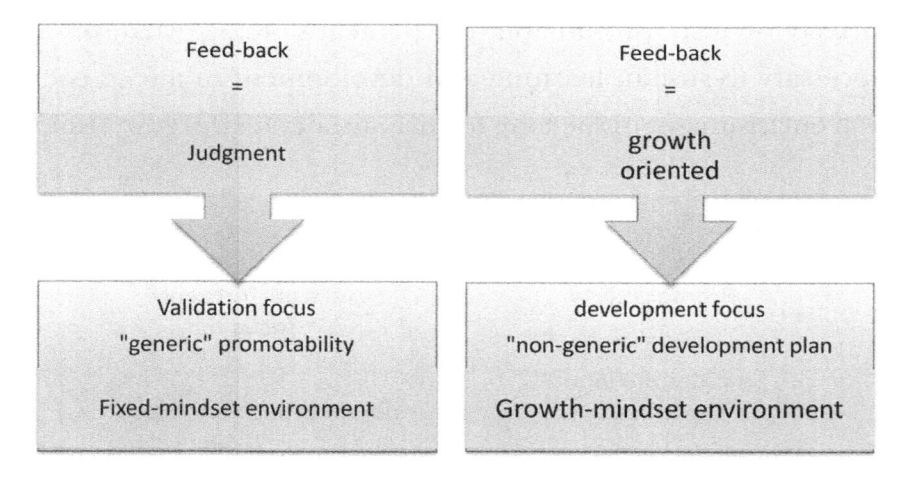

Feed-back = Judgment	Feed-back = growth oriented
Validation focus "generic" promotability	development focus "non-generic" development plan
Fixed-mindset environment	Growth-mindset environment

This difference in <u>how</u> feed-back is given can be essential for the learning and development process within organizations, with important effects on motivation and climate. Both companies have a developmental approach, Company Y however makes it clear that the whole process is a learning process : mistakes are part of the learning experience, it's not just a matter of "bouncing back quickly from disappointment and mistakes".

A Human Resources Director working for a Pharmaceutical Group made an interesting remark about this promotion-oriented approach. She defined it as being "short-sighted", since the tendency organizations are experiencing is to have flatter hierarchies (hierarchies de plus en plus plates), matrix structures and more project-oriented careers than hierarchy oriented career paths. Those organizational changes permit them to react more quickly to a changing environment. The "up two levels" promotion approach, she said, is beginning to lose its meaning when it comes to define high-potentials. The future seems much more about learning fast, adapting and adjusting quickly then about stepping up levels. Daniel Pink (2009) makes an interesting remark about future organizational trends when considering intrinsic motivational theories: "*as organizations flatten, companies need people who are self-motivated. That forces many organizations to become more like open source projects. Nobody sits around trying to figure out how to "motivate" them. That's why Linux, and Wikipedia and Firefox work.*" Besides what has been mentioned above, looking at <u>how</u> feedback is applied, organizations have very different approaches and these trends might contribute to change. In most cases it's hierarchy-oriented. What do we mean by it? First of all it can be applied either top-down, bottom-up or both. Top-down means that the boss gives feedback to his direct reports and during the people review the higher hierarchy gives feedback on those that are "below" (N-1 and N-2), discussing their performance, attitudes and behaviors and those that use the 9-box-grid, putting them in the appropriate box. If the feedback is "one-way", if it is applied only in one direction, top-down in this case, can we really call it a "feedback" culture? The further up in the hierarchy a person will get, the less feedback he/she will receive. It's

The Name of the Game

about evaluating and assessing systematically how you behave as a "*subject*", if we are to use monarchical terms; as if how you behave as a boss wasn't relevant, as if the subject's perspective was not of interest. The higher you get the more "immunity" you will gain. Shouldn't it be the other way around? Shouldn't it be: the higher you get, the more responsibilities you have, the more you need feedback to be in resonance (*R.Boyatzis, A.McKee, Resonant Leadership, 2005*) with the organization you are leading? 85% of the organizations reported having a one-way, top-down feedback approach. None reported only bottom-up feedback and 15% reported two-way, top-down and bottom up 360 degrees feedback. In addition to data, reactions were very different to this question. Some couldn't possibly imagine a "two-way" feedback approach; others were sincerely intrigued by the possibility of bottom-up feedback and started questioning how this could be put in place. One of the HR Directors questioned the use of a two-way feedback because of its possible "demagogical" consequences. This depends on the organizational culture: if it's a validation-oriented culture it's better not to take the risk. In this case there would be a gap between rhetoric and reality and it would be quickly perceived by employees. If you believe in "natural talent", in fixed-traits, the fact that you move up in hierarchy is the proof that you are "better than others", in this case why should you need feedback from below? In the fixed-mindset environment, the feedback from below is just something the boss might use to his/her own personal advantage (and to others' disadvantage if necessary). A fixed-mindset environment is an environment where people tend to benchmark themselves against others, instead of benchmarking their own progress. The HR Group Talent Development Director that applied the two-way feed-back approach reported it was a huge success. It was introduced quite recently, and he applied it because he learned how to apply this process in the previous organization he worked for. In both organizations it worked very well, he reported. He found it particularly useful when managers integrated a new team, it made the integration process smoother and everybody adjusted much faster, since they learned from mistakes given that <u>both</u> parties were open to feed-back. Openness to feedback makes it possible to learn from mistakes, to avoid vicious circles and motivation drops, and helps everybody learn in order to adjust faster. If you adjust faster, you have a better chance of performing better. The fact of knowing that stepping up won't give "immunity", means that humility is one of the key-values of the organization's culture. People remain open and value effort and learning. This bottom-up feedback process has become such a success within his organization, reported the Head of Talent Development Director, that they are having a hard time keeping up with demand. As with any evaluation, this process also needs training to be applied effectively.

TO BE OR NOT TO BE? TO TELL OR NOT TO TELL?

Feed-back means to provide information on how a person did in terms of what was done and on how it was performed. It's about being as <u>specific</u> as possible. To tell people whether they are or aren't on a high-potential list shouldn't be interpreted as a lack of feed-back or lack of transparency. High-potential is a future projection, you cannot possibly be transparent about something you yourself do not know (unless you have a crystal ball). What you are making is an inference based on an infinite number of variables, it's a bet. You cannot supply transparency on a bet. If the choice of telling high-potentials they have been identified and selected is justified by a transparency "moral imperative", it is a bit odd, if not a paradox. What do organizations do? Do they communicate to their top-talent pool that they have been identified and selected as high-potentials? If they do, how do they communicate this information? Many consulting companies wrote articles that sustain the importance of telling high-potentials they are identified and selected (Korn Ferry, M.Lombardo and Robert W. Eichinger, or M. Campbell and R. Smith in Center for Creative Leadership), however none of these papers gives the slightest cue about how and when it should be done, nor of how it should be communicated. The guided interview contained various questions about this topic - i.e. telling or not telling high-potentials they are on a list - that should be useful to better understand the why, when and how of this exercise. Besides, it was interesting to know what Human Resources Directors thought and felt personally about this topic. An overview of the policies first permits to get an idea of what organizations do :

POTENTIAL IN DIFFERENT GAMES

	What term is employed to define this population?	Are High potentials formally told they are on the list?	Are there special programs dedicated only to High-potentials?
Company A	Capacity to Grow	NO	YES
Company B	Best Bets, Next Generation	NO YES: only if succession plan	YES
Company C	A-players	NO	YES
Company D	High-Potentials: (4 categories)	NO (unless people want to know)	YES
Company E	Evolving Key-talents	NO	YES
Company F	–	NO	NO
Company G	High-Potentials and Very High Potentials	YES	YES
Company H	Rising Talents	NO	TBD
Company I	–	NO	YES
Company J	High-Potentials	NO	YES
Company K	Talents, Rising Stars	NO	YES
Company L	Emerging candidate	NO	YES
Company M	High-Potentials, 3 categories (3, 2B, 2A, 1)	YES (every division is free to decide, it's a management choice)	YES
Company N	High-Potentials	YES (since 2012)	YES
Company O	High-Potentials	YES	YES

If Company D counts as negative (because the company policy decided not to tell high-potentials about their status, although people can ask and get the information if they want), and Company O counts as positive (because high-potential talent being strictly inscribed in a succession planning process is informed about future options), in this case 75% of the organizations are against formally telling high-potentials they have been identified and selected and are on a special radar-screen.

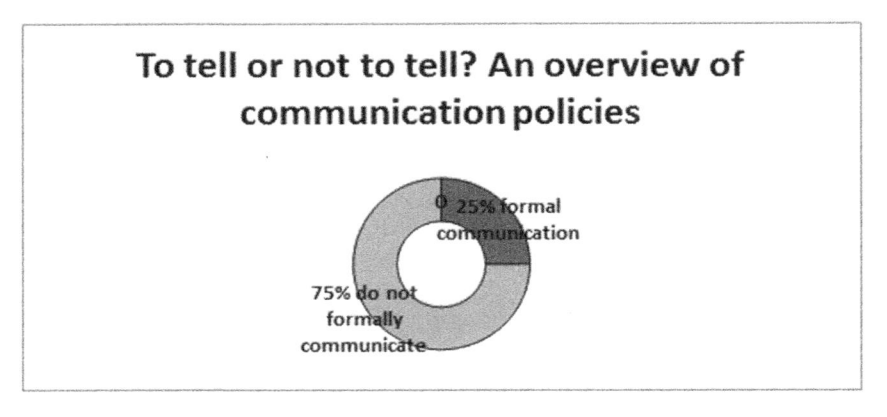

To tell or not to tell? An overview of communication policies

- 25% formal communication
- 75% do not formally communicate

However, what is interesting besides the policies is to have a closer look at the practices. Looking closer at those practices, it is never completely black or white; there are interesting grey-areas. The grey-area is everything between telling and not telling, or disclosing the information to a certain category of high-potentials and not to another. Practices can vary from company to company and the grey-areas give interesting insights into the company's culture. A HR Director said that the grey-areas arise when communication becomes a delicate issue, which is the case when it comes to questions like "to tell or not to tell?" or "how to tell them"? He said that the question that should be asked is not a communication issue, but rather an equity and justice issue. In this case the impression is that communication is just a way to try to make it appear "less ugly", a way to force the pill down as smoothly as possible. In many companies for example, and it won't come to most of you as a surprise, there are special development programs that are intended and destined only to the high-potential population. In this case an HR Director laughed saying "the person must be really dumb if he/she doesn't figure it out!" In fact, many companies decided not to communicate formally about it, however developed special programs for those selected few. Another HR Director said that the "long-term high-potentials" don't know they are on the list and do not have special programs, they have development programs just like everyone else. Long-term high potentials are the younger generation, those with less than 8-10 years-work experience. In this company, the only ones that are formally informed and have access to special programs are those that are on a succession planning list. In this case the term potential is specific, there is a (more or less) clearly defined position the person is retained for. The question "potential what for?" has a specific answer. The policy in this company, interestingly, is not to communicate who is on the list. Nevertheless, the decision of telling specific individuals that they are on a 'succession planning" list makes sense. The meaning lies in the fact, explained the HR Director, that there is a long-term high-potential population that needs to be tested on the job in the medium to long-term before being granted access to broader responsibilities, they don't need to know they are on a list. In contrast there are individuals that are meant to take broader responsibilities in a short time-span, they are on a succession planning list, and in such a specific context they should know we are considering them and counting on them, besides the fact that : "we have to discuss with them the opportunity and check their interest and motivation". He explained that they prefer not telling the 'long-term' high-potentials (or next-generation)

The Name of the Game

they are on the list for two reasons: avoiding labels for equity reasons among employees (those that are and those that aren't on the list), and to avoid frustration for those that might exit the list after a given period of time. First, although the term equity is usually used to describe J. Stacy Adam's theory (J.Stacy Adams, 1963), it is at least as appropriate to describe it as inequity theory. The major motivating force considered is a striving for equity, but some degree of inequity must be perceived before this force can be mobilized. If an organization creates a label 'high-potential', an HR Director explained, that implies that "the others are something different than 'high-potential' and not necessarily better, if you see what I mean. This creates unease, a sense of inequity in the majority of the population that feels under-valued". Inequity, when perceived, results in dissatisfaction either in the form of anger, frustration, demotivation (under-reward) or guilt (over-reward) (in John B Miner, Organizational Behaviour 1, 2005). The high-potential won't feel a sense of guilt, they will rarely feel over-rewarded, they will feel a sense of satisfaction and even some pride; while the others (which is in most cases over 95% of the company's population) will have a feeling of frustration, if not anger. Be it frustration for many, be it pride for a few (having C.S. Dweck's mindsets theory in mind), in both cases consequences are not encouraging. Below are some HR Directors' personal positions and feelings when asked this question:

COMPANY A: *"I am personally not in favour of communicating to the CTG (capacity to grow population) that they are on the list, since it often depends upon the context and options that are open at a given moment. Key is to ask 'potential what for'? It can be identified*

POTENTIAL IN DIFFERENT GAMES

according to a given opportunity and it can disappear depending upon different factors and a multitude of variables. That's why in our organization the CGT population is not managed apart, they are within our talent management practice. By that I mean that we don't have a parallel or superimposed system dedicated only to less than 10% of the population".

COMPANY B: *"I would be personally in favour of telling people they are high potentials only for the short-term-high-potential category, since there is a contingency situation. Short-term is always linked to succession planning. Also in this case it should be a HR professional who tells them in the right way, in order to avoid frustration. In this short-term HP category, if the person doesn't perform as expected we have strong development programs, training and feedbacks to help fill gaps. For the other HP categories I am clearly against telling. If you aren't on the list any longer it's a source of great frustration and de-motivation".*

COMPANY C: *"In my personal opinion high-potentials shouldn't be told they are on the list because this would mean creating unnecessary expectations that might be frustrated for contingency reasons".*

COMPANY D: *"Personally against telling, even if in our organization people can have access to the information if they want to. Even if we put everybody in the 9 matrix grid, it's not carved in stone. It's not a matter of 'acquired status'. However, it is not easy to communicate about it in a growth oriented way".*

COMPANY E: *"We do not communicate about who is on the list, they do not know. They might deduce it however because they are invited to training programs, or to have lunch with a senior executive, or to be*

The Name of the Game

on a project team with other key-talent members. But they don't ever get confirmation about being or not key-talent. We have a discussion every year about this subject during the executive committee meeting. Every year there are people that strive to make the information public and this year, as every year, the decision was taken against it. I would like to have some strong arguments against it personally, since I think it's a bad idea. It risks demotivating many, and on the other hand we could create a bunch of arrogant executives with big egos. Besides the fact that we risk spoiling their talent and motivation by creating expectations that won't ever be fulfilled in the way they imagine or expect. That means to deal with frustration later on. The perverse effects of telling are too great in my point of view".

COMPANY F: *"In my point of view, when we really know how to manage talent, we will avoid this "one way trap" of "high-potentials / low potential approach". At that point we will really be able to estimate potential (everyone's potential) and define it in terms of ability versus wishes and ambition. We have a hard time evaluating personal versus professional commitment, growth commitment is strictly related to this sphere".*

THE HIGH POTENTIAL "ONE WAY TRAP"

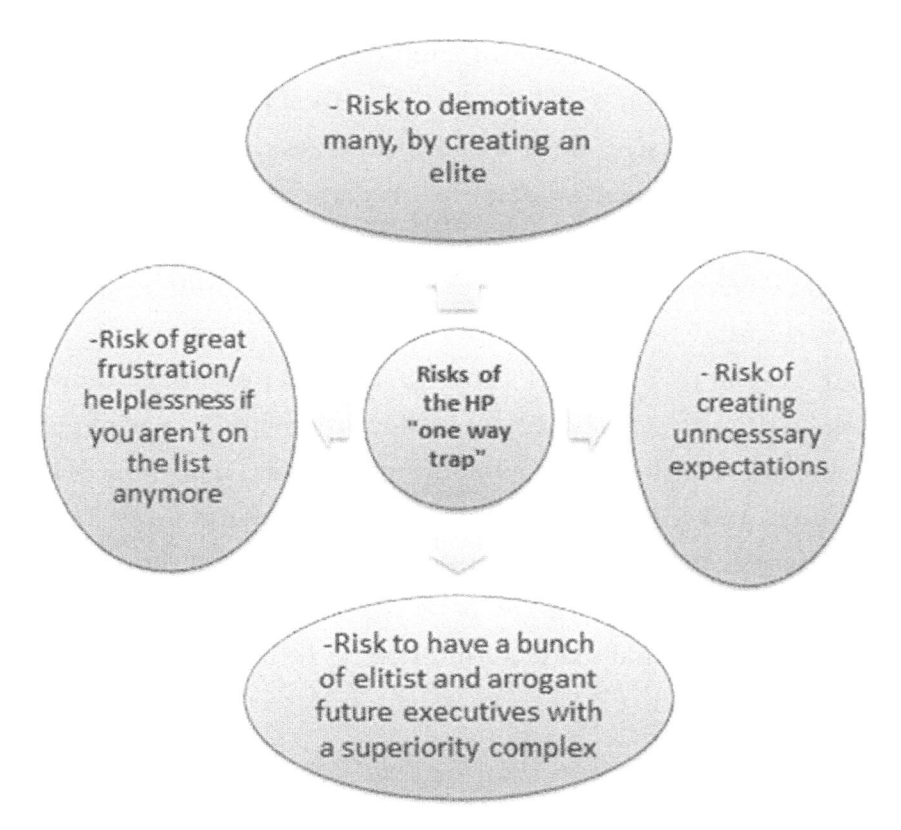

- Risk to demotivate many, by creating an elite

- Risk of great frustration/helplessness if you aren't on the list anymore

Risks of the HP "one way trap"

- Risk of creating unncesssary expectations

- Risk to have a bunch of elitist and arrogant future executives with a superiority complex

Almost 75% of the organizations that keep the high-potential lists confidential actually do have special training and leadership development programs for this population. They do not communicate officially, but they still let them know. They avoid confirming a "status" and wish nevertheless to give a growth-oriented message. They avoid putting the focus on validation.

The Name of the Game

Twenty per cent of the companies reported they communicate officially to high-potentials they are on the list and besides, invite them to special development programs. We can find the opposite situation too: a company that does not have a high-potential approach to talent, however they have a "milestone career" system (step up from level 3 to level 2 and so forth) that requires special leadership development programs and assessments. Only one organization reported a policy that avoids labels and any kind of elitism, be it confirmed or unconfirmed. They decided recently to suppress *dedicated* programs to any kind of 'talent category'. Now their high-potentials cannot deduce they are on a list because they are invited to participate in special training or leadership programs. They do have trainings and leadership programs, but these are always open to different talent categories, in such a way that there is no place for elitism. Below is the personal position of an Executive Talent Director that made an interesting reflection on her life-long experience:

COMPANY G: *You have high-potential programs when you need good officers that perform and act according to expectations. Good officers need validation. In my point of view leaders don't need to be motivated by external factors, they motivate themselves, they have a vision. Perhaps good officers are all companies need and want nowadays. However I personally think that companies if they want to be competitive in the 21st century, they must give a chance to creativity and team effort. "High-potential" is a fairly individual approach to talent and in my career I have witnessed that high-potentials were often very 'formatted'. Besides the fact that there is the effect of pride once they know they are 'chosen' that makes them sometimes blind to mistakes and arrogant. In case a high-potential is informed that he/she isn't on the list anymore we have often witnessed de-motivation, but sometimes worse, a feeling of helplessness from which it is difficult to recover".*

There are, on the other hand, HR Directors who are in favour of communicating to high-potentials that they are identified and selected. There are two kinds of arguments that are used frequently to support transparency.

1. The first is a motivational argument. It presupposes that knowing you are one of the selected few is a source of stronger motivation.

2. The second is a retention argument, meaning that if high-potentials know they are identified and selected, they will be less inclined to leave the company.

The HR Group Talent Director of a large organization reported this was a theme that was heavily debated during the last executive committee "*on whether to go transparent or not*". Supported by the argument that high-potentials knew anyway (because of dedicated training and leadership development programs), they decided to let them know officially. The counter-arguments to this motivation- and retention-focused approach are the following ones:

- High-potentials are not supposed to need a label or external motivation to move forward

- Officially or unofficially high-potential, if not given opportunities to learn and stretch, there are no labels that should retain them, and if they do, that means that they are not really high-potentials.

A third argument, which is hypothetical, however based on intrinsic and extrinsic motivation theories (E.L. Deci et al. 1971), would suggest that if you promise a reward you tend to decrease motivation and performance instead of increasing it. "Rewards can deliver a short-term boost, but effects wears off and, worse, can reduce a person's longer-term motivation to continue the project" (Daniel Pink, 2007).

A Group HR Training and Talent Development Director explained why he is in favor of telling high-potentials they are on the radar screen:

"I am in favour of telling without ambiguity. This helps putting some pressure on both. It's a way to retain them and motivate them and the company also has to engage and provide options. It's a win-win process in my opinion. Concerning equity I don't really know, nevertheless as long as rules are clearly set everything should be fine. The only problem I can raise is about subjectivity. In our organization the managers, the operational executives are those that identify and select, they are the ones involved in assessment and their opinion is at times really subjective".

Practices and policies may seem more or less equitable or just, nevertheless what will always come first are the organization's needs. If the company needs good officers to assure performance in a rough economic period they might make a good choice by choosing "be-good" profiles and give employees a 'be-good" focus. If they need innovation to ensure the company's survival and face complex and first-time situations, they might be keener to select their high-potential employees differently, according to creativity and entrepreneurial skills and give them a 'get-better' focus. There is no right or wrong, however there is a better- , or even best approach depending on the organization's goals. These goals should be always measured in the short-, medium and long-term. Negative consequences on motivation due to inequity can take a long time to be reversed, that's why decisions should be taken carefully and unnecessary risks should be avoided. What can be an unnecessary risk? A striking aspect about these policies and practices dedicated to high-potentials is to just focus on rates:

- How many high-potentials are there compared to total population (percentage rate)?

- What is the recovery rate every year? (how many high-potentials exit the list and how many new ones enter)?

High potentials represent in some cases 10 % of total population (Company A and B), others report having between 1 and 5 % (Company E:5%, G:1%, I:5%, J:3%, M: 1,2%), while others report a much higher rate that reaches up to 20 % of total population (Company D and N; D having 13 % high-potentials plus 7% key-contributors or experts). Some said that they thought 5% too few, while others said that 1,2 % was already too much. Too much or too little compared to what? What should be an adequate percentage rate of a high-potential population? There is no recipe. If the company has a talent approach, they identify those that correspond to the company's needs and don't need to share who is on and who is off the list.

The Name of the Game

There is no 'list' approach, there is constant observation and everybody passes under a magnifying glass, there is no such thing as a pool of "usual suspects". There are companies that have a large pool of high-potentials (up to 20 %) and give a chance to people on a wider basis, they test them on the job and the best ones step up, while others are removed from list as time passes; other companies that perceive the downside of the game, the possible perverse effects, prefer to be extremely selective, they have a very small high-potential talent pool and measure the recovery rate tightly (if it's above 1 per cent that means that there is something going wrong on in the selection process). "*A high recovery rate*", reported the HR Director of the company that decided to go transparent recently, "*is a delicate issue in the future, since we risk demotivating a large number of employees in the long-term if we don't assess properly, especially having a large percentage of high-potential population (between 10-20 per cent)*". At the moment they have a recovery rate of approximately 1 per cent, "*it's important*", she added, "*that once we go transparent, this recovery rate drops*". Moreover they have to elaborate and deploy a clear communication policy about how to tell people they are selected and to those that are off the list, that they are unfortunately not retained. Other companies reported recovery rates between 5 and 15%.

If we now compare recovery rates, the picture which emerges is quite striking. Some companies reported having calculated a recovery rate in high potential list of up to 60%! Company J reported a recovery rate between 2009 and 2010 of 60 % (meaning that 60% of the High-potential list changed from one year to the next). Company E reported a recovery rate of 30%.

POTENTIAL IN DIFFERENT GAMES

The HR Director of company E explained "*We have a hierarchical list of key-talent, they are not stable lists, it changes every year and we have a recovery rate of about 30%. Besides, we have an official list that is communicated to the Group HR Director and a unofficial list that we keep under our radar screen and which enables us to observe closely those that are not in, about whom we might have a doubt. This high recovery rate is not traumatic, because our high-potentials are not told they are on the list. That's why I don't want to create expectations and then take the risk of frustrating them*". It's obvious that if you have 60% recovery rate on your high-potential list, it's not a good idea to go transparent, unless employees get so used to getting on and off the list that it's a trauma they get accustomed to.

The first misleading impression was that the higher the recovery rate, the worse the talent management practice and their selection skills. Thus, the first erroneous thought was that selection was not done properly. However, it is not a matter of right or wrong selection, since the needs of the company evolve, strategies as well as business priorities change and variables linked to employees also change over time. What might have been a need and a rare skill three years ago might not be one today. Furthermore, the larger the pool the better it is, on the one hand a greater risk of having many people getting out of the list sooner or later, on the other hand a greater chance of avoiding neglecting a rare pearl that was not in the "usual suspect pool" from the beginning. And last of all, the fact that this misleading first thought about a "too high recovery rate" might derive from a fixed-mindset approach. Do we really want a stable pool? What in fact does a stable high-potential pool mean? It means taking the risk to create a fixed-mindset environment in which either you are a "natural" or you aren't, either you are in or you are out. The growth-mindset, on the other hand, is based on the belief that your basic qualities are things you can cultivate through your efforts, where "becoming is better than being". The fixed-mindset does not allow people the luxury of becoming. In a fixed-mindset environment it's crucial to be perfect right now, because one test, one evaluation, can measure you forever. Thus, the smaller the pool and the more stable it is, if you communicate who is on the list, the higher the risk of creating a fixed-mindset environment.

A RISKY RECIPE

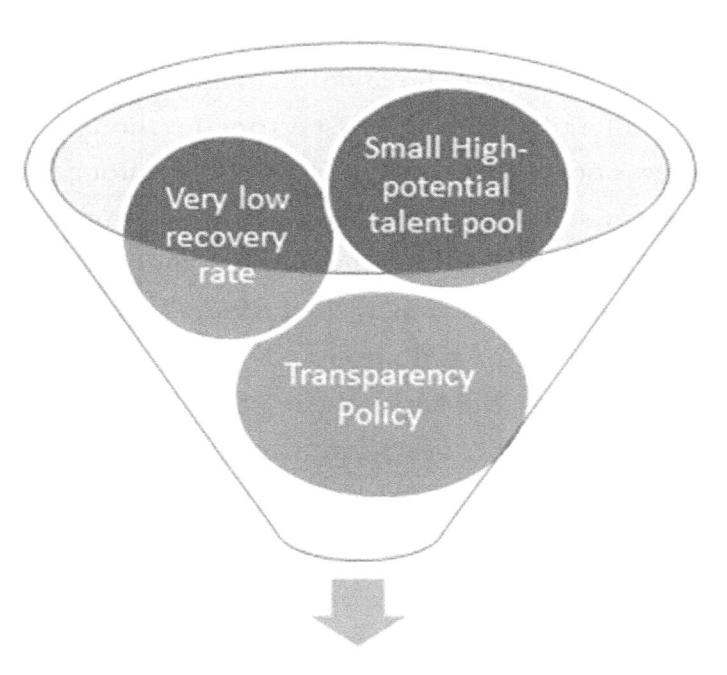

(Funnel diagram containing: "Very low recovery rate", "Small High-potential talent pool", "Transparency Policy", with arrow pointing down to:)

Risk of creating a Fixed-Mindset Environment

POTENTIAL IN DIFFERENT GAMES

People that are shifted into a fixed-mindset environment, as we saw in the previous chapters, tend to prove themselves over and over again, they have to prove they are smart and every situation calls for a confirmation. In a fixed-mindset environment people tend to avoid taking risks, exposing themselves and acknowledging mistakes, because in this kind of culture "if at first you don't succeed, you probably don't have the ability". Dweck reports that when in her experiments she put (even only temporarily) people in a fixed-mindset, with its focus on permanent traits, they quickly devalue effort and it was proven that they became also terrible at estimating their abilities (self-assessment). It makes sense, if you think you are on a list that is almost 'carved in stone' containing the "very best" – *la crème de la crème* - you better prove it over and over again and you have a good chance of becoming super-sensitive about being wrong or making mistakes, since it means you are not smart or talented enough.

The fixed-mindset is what might in fact lead people not to fulfilling their potential. Benjamin Barber, an eminent sociologist, once said *"I don't divide the world into the weak and the strong, or the successes and the failures. I divide the world into the learners and the non-learners"*. Various HR Directors made the remark that "learning agility" (see M.Lombardo and R. Eichinger, *High Potentials as high-learners*, 2000) is one of the most important variables that define potential. One of them said *"Potential is fundamentally about learning, growing and adapting. Learning fast and adapting smoothly."*

DIFFERENT MODELS

When should potential be identified and assessed? Organizations did not give an age range. All of them reported that potential evaluation is an on-going process that is regularly discussed during the Annual Interview with the employee, which is followed by the Annual Talent Review (some call it Annual People Review, others Succession Planning Council). Some HR Directors affirmed they still had high potentials at the age of 50, while others affirmed that above the age of 45-50 there wasn't any high-potential category in the organization. Some companies have different high-potential categories according to work experience and acquired competencies (how many years of experience); others focus more on scope and responsibilities. In the first approach seniority and experience play a greater role compared to the second approach. Moreover, there are companies that give special importance to "career milestones", what can be called "critical promotion" to a senior executive responsibilities position (i.e. in some companies the milestone promotion can be called "Executive band", or up to "Level 1", or up to Level 17). The companies that focus on scope and responsibilities tend to admit that the age range to access these "milestone positions" varies between 35 and 45 years old. Companies that don't have career "milestones" references tend in general to be more open to consider potential at any given age, but there are some exceptions. The companies that don't have a high-potential program (approach), reported having either a career milestone model or an experience oriented model, also in this case age seemed to be more critical in the career 'milestone' model.

An HR Director made an interesting reflection: "*My personal conviction about key-talent, is that it is not a matter of age, especially now that people tend to retire late, well over the age of 60. A person could be a key-talent at the age of fifty or more. However on paper key-talent is usually between 35 and 45*". Another indicator given by another HR Director was about how long it takes to assess potential. In his organization he said they devote at least three years to careful observation before somebody is identified as Rising Talent. Most companies reported that observing people on-the-job is the main assessment tool. They observe both behaviour and achievement (delivery) on the job. One HR Director reported observing one thing in particular: how the potential "rising stars" react to negative feed-back. Either they listen to the negative feed-back, accept it and take it as a learning opportunity, or they react by giving excuses and finding external justification for what went wrong. This, he explained, is one of the important aspects that must be checked when assessing potential. A Human Resources Director that came from another organization compared his previous organizational high-potential management model to the current one saying: "*the previous talent management model was much more High-Potential focused, compared to the present company I am working for. By that I mean that they were looking for charismatic people with excellent education.*" In this case as the HR Talent Development Director of Company K the assessment effort is done at the very beginning, at the hiring. But while

The Name of the Game

in the first case it's a matter of hiring the "best in class"; in the second case assessment beyond education is carried out during the first years on the job. In the first case, time is the validation variable or tool; in the second case, the focus is rather on effort, development, adaptability and fitting to the organization's values. Another HR Director reported having had until a few years ago a high-potential talent pool that was composed of employees in an age range of 29-34 years old, then they decided to stretch it to 40 (also due to the fact that women in this age range often take maternity leave and risk being left out of the process). The impression is that the tighter you set the rules, the smaller the talent pools are, the more you strive to crunch the recovery rates, the more you limit age ranges, the more you worry about keeping it fuzzy …. the more you get caught in contradictions and perverse consequences. This approach that tends to limit and control the variables, gives only an illusory impression of control. The difficulty is fighting what can be a reassuring but illusory impression of control, embracing a wider possibility of options, but at the same time that won't limit drastically the chances of success eluding so many options and possibilities. A senior HR Director sustained that he never witnessed a high-potential model, meaning a separated and superimposed High-potential management structure on the talent management practice, work "*beyond the first year*". Separate management of high-potentials proved to be in his experience a failure, he never believed in this approach, but often saw aborted attempts. The big challenge, he said, is to create a consistent and effective talent management model. He stressed the importance of consistency, saying that when *"the communication policy about talent management becomes essential, it means that it's already a palliative therapy for negative side-effect"*. The central question that should be asked is not about communication (how and when to communicate), but about equity and justice. If it is complex and you have to think about when and how to tell something, if at all, it is because something went wrong. Consequences and side-effects weren't accurately weighed up.

Beyond the questions related to assessment, the "What" (achievement, delivery, objectives) and the "How" (behaviours, attitudes and values) of potential discussed above, a HR Director sustained that the challenge nowadays is rather to find ways to better prepare key-talent for what lies ahead. He said : *"What lies ahead is getting more and more complex, things change fast (markets, trends, technologies) and experiences are becoming not merely more complex but also more <u>intense</u>. Intensity is difficult to handle in the long-run. Until recently there were different ways to prepare key-talent for this future complexity. The "classic approach" has been stretch-assignments, international experiences, special-projects, changing functions, transversal assignments and so forth. This approach however doesn't seem to be enough, it doesn't correspond to our present needs"*. What he meant is to continue with the "classic approach" to developing skills on the job over a given period of time, but adding what he called a *"experience in a pill"*. The "pill experiences" are condensed experiences that are added to the current functions of the employee, but aren't inscribed in the same hierarchical line. It's about working with a group of people that have certain affinities (ex. Sales from different divisions and different countries) on a condensed project that

The Name of the Game

creates a 'community' and added value. The strength of this idea is that it creates intensity, because the current functions are held at the same time as the project (or pill experience). The employee learns to deal with two vectors at the same time, thus having higher work intensity. It reminds Daniel Coyle's description of the secret of Brazilian football talent: football de salão. Futsal is a more condensed version of football, here players have to deal with many more stimuli at the same time in less space (D. Coyle, *The talent code, 2009*).

Another important question that was discussed during the interviews was about who carries out the assessment. Who assesses potential? There are three main options that were described in more or less detail, some more development oriented, others more assessment oriented, some more centralized, while others more decentralized. The de-centralized model leaves great autonomy on this subject to businesses. Depending upon the organizational structure and culture we find three situations:

1. Managers assess potential, and they have the final word (HR are there for taking in charge the process).

2. HR professionals assess potential, working hand in hand with mangers, having the final word (discussions involving many people, in some companies minimum of 8).

3. A consulting company, an external assessor, is in charge of validating and confirming what has been observed over the years.

POTENTIAL IN DIFFERENT GAMES

When operational managers are in charge of potential assessment, HR Directors reported sometimes having serious doubts about the "subjectivity" of the assessment. The HR Director of a Financial Institution made an interesting remark: *"Managers are those who spend ten hours a day with their people, they are the ones that see how they perform. Here lies the problem of the assessment, since they are more performance-focused than competency focused. It's very difficult to know if their assessment concerning current abilities versus "future abilities" can be trusted. Besides, subjectivity is an additional issue"*. Furthermore, if managers are the assessors of potential, it is important to take into account their mindset (their IPTs -implicit person theory). Holding the fixed-mindset assumption, that human attributes are innate and unalterable can make people disinclined to invest in developmental initiatives, such as providing ideas and inspiration to help others improve. We saw in Silzer and Church (2009) and in Groysberg et al. (2004) that they emphasize how employees' latent potential may not be unleashed or manifest if they are working in an insufficiently supportive and challenging environment. In two field studies (Heslin, VandeWallle and Latham 2006) they observed that the extent to which managers held a growth mindset significantly predicted the extent of their employee coaching. Related insights are given on the role of manager's mindsets in how they appraise employee performance. Because a fixed mindset involves presuming that other people generally do not change, Erdley and Dweck (1993) theorized and found that compared to those with a growth-mindset, children with a fixed mindset held more rigid initial impressions of their classmates, assigning relatively strong evaluative labels and not seeking additional information to test their initial impressions, what's more they tended to quickly stereotype others (Levy, Stroessner & Dweck 1998), they tended to ignore information that was inconsistent with their first impressions and with their stereotypes (Gervey, Chiu, Hong and Dweck 1999) and personal expectations (Mangels, Butterfield, Lamb, Good & Dweck 2006; Molden, Plaks and Dweck, 2006). The results of this study were confirmed by further studies on older populations. In an organizational context Heslin, Latham & VandeWalle (2005) observed that the extent to which managers held a growth mindset predicted more accurately their employees performance (be it improvement or decline). What their research showed is that, despite the fact that pessimism about the malleability of employees' potential is prevalent among organizations and consulting firms, there is a meaningful variation in managers' assumptions about malleability – and that this variation has implications for how they cultivate and assess employees. There are three sets of issues worth relating (Heslin, 2006): the first evidence regarding how managers' mindset is associated with the quantity and quality of the employee coaching they provide, suggests that managers with a fixed mindset are unlikely to provide employees with a development context in which their potential may flourish. Second, initial performances are often not accurate predictors of what an individual is ultimately capable of achieving (Dweck 2006). Thus, the inclination of managers with a fixed mindset to make relatively rigid snap judgments of employees may lead to both "false alarms and misses" (Heslin 2009) in the identification of potential. Meaning that, should evidence emerge that initial assessments of high potential are not warranted, managers with a growth mindset are more likely than those with a fixed mindset to update their initial 'overly rosy' judgment of potential, and inversely, identify potential that they haven't noticed in the beginning, thus revising their first impression. The third, derived from the above, suggests that fixed mindset managers might lead to more misses in the identification of employee potential. Furthermore, a managers' fixed mindset might be mediated through what Davidson and Eden (2000) called the *Golem effect* in their article "Remedial self-fulfilling prophecy", whereby they acknowledged that high-potential employees internalize and then act in accordance with their manager's fixed mindset applying the same rules, attitudes and behaviors (in the same way as Dweck showed how easy it is to make people slide into a fixed- or developmental mindset). Consideration of the assessor's mindset would be important when deploying a high-potential identification model.

The potential assessment model should measure the assessed- as well as the assessor's mindset, and special caution is suggested about validity of the assessments of employee potential provided by managers with a strong fixed mindset, unless it is a conscious choice of seeking a validation culture with a strong performance focus. If it's not the case, then providing growth mindset training to those with a fixed mindset who are charged with indentifying employees' potential is an important aspect to be kept in mind.

When the process is in the hands of Human Resources Specialists it represents a huge effort of data collection, reference taking (some do 360 degree evaluation and

The Name of the Game

feedback and share results), job listing and calibration which provides an overview of the talent pool. The result of this effort is presented and discussed with operational managers during the annual People review. Many reported that potential assessment is collectively discussed and decision isn't taken unless at least eight people are present and agree on the employee's assessment. Twelve out of fifteen organizations reported not using neither psychometrics nor assessment centers. Of those three, one reported using the Hogan evaluation, but with a development- and not an assessment goal; while the two other organizations reported turning to external consulting companies to assess senior-executives (potential executive committee level). One Company reports having too many assessment methods and scales and relies on their leadership model. Another company uses two assessment "drivers": the first is the "net promotion score" (developed by Bain & Co) which refers to what the clients/customers think about the job you do; the second is the "engagement index" which refers to how ready the person is to go the extra mile and engage people to reach the objective. Derailing factors are mainly behavioural, most HR Directors affirmed. However, QE assessment is something that has been very recently introduced (or is in progress of introduction in models and processes) in more than 20% of the approached organizations. Furthermore, more than 20% of the approached organizations selected the services of external assessors and affirmed paying particular attention to whether the consulting company included 'learning agility' in their potential-assessment model or not.

POTENTIAL IN DIFFERENT GAMES

To the question: is potential an inborn trait or acquired? HR Directors answered mostly by saying that it is a mixture of both, but the percentage of the mix varied sensitively. 85% of the interviewees affirmed that in their opinion potential was mostly acquired and in some lesser degree innate. 15% of the HR Directors that affirmed that potential is *mostly inborn*, said that it is a personality trait that is difficult to acquire. The HR Directors that affirmed that potential is *mostly acquired* said that they believe that people can change in most aspects, except **ambition, motivation and drive**. One of the HR Directors made an interesting comment to the question, saying that more than a question about innate and acquired, which is his point of view too generic, it's about assessing the *level of self-awareness* and other personality traits when the person enters the organization and how fast he/she can grow, pointing to the fact that past experiences and background count a lot.

When asked to name three key-high potential factors besides motivation, they answered differently.

Here below a few answers:

- *Learning agility, cognitive capacities (skills and competencies) and Emotional intelligence,* described as the capacity to connect to others, bringing the best out of people.

- *Learning agility, drive to excel, entrepreneurial spirit.*

- Another HR Director named *resilience, leadership and drive.*

The Name of the Game

- *Managing complexity (cognitive, calculated risk taking), managing uncertainty (insight), ability to develop relations (QE=engaging others)*

- *Ambition, QE (related to oneself = self-awareness and related to others=empathy) and Energy (leader not follower).*

If most qualities and competencies can be learned, leaders have the responsibility of creating and supporting the development of talent and of the future generation of leaders. The message of McCall in his book "High Flyers: developing the next generation of leaders" is that leadership ability can be learned, that creating a context that supports the development of talent can become a source of competitive advantage, and that the development of leaders is itself a "leadership responsibility". Goethe wrote *"Treat people as if they were what they ought to be and you help them to become what they are capable of being"*. Goethe's view has been confirmed by social psychology works such as McClelland (1966), Seligman and Maier (1967), and Albert Bandura's experiments. All demonstrate the role other's expectations and examples play in shaping individuals' interests, drives, and beliefs about their own abilities (Dominick and Gabriel, 2009). Implicit theories concern individuals as much as organizations. If leaders and human resources executives are conscious of this implicit framework, they will be able to make appropriate choices and match their talented employees to their strategies and goals. They will know what kind of potential to look for. If a company's business is based on following the same patterns over and over again and work is mostly performance focused, the fact of selecting fixed mindset employees could represent a good strategy. To hire growth-mindset

POTENTIAL IN DIFFERENT GAMES

employees in a fixed mindset-environment would be a mistake. The growth mindset employees would perceive they are not learning, they would feel frustrated within months, because the validation and the 'be good' focus would not bring satisfaction (See Figure below). On the contrary, if the company's business is a more entrepreneurial model that needs constant innovation, it is important to hire and/or develop growth-mindset talent.

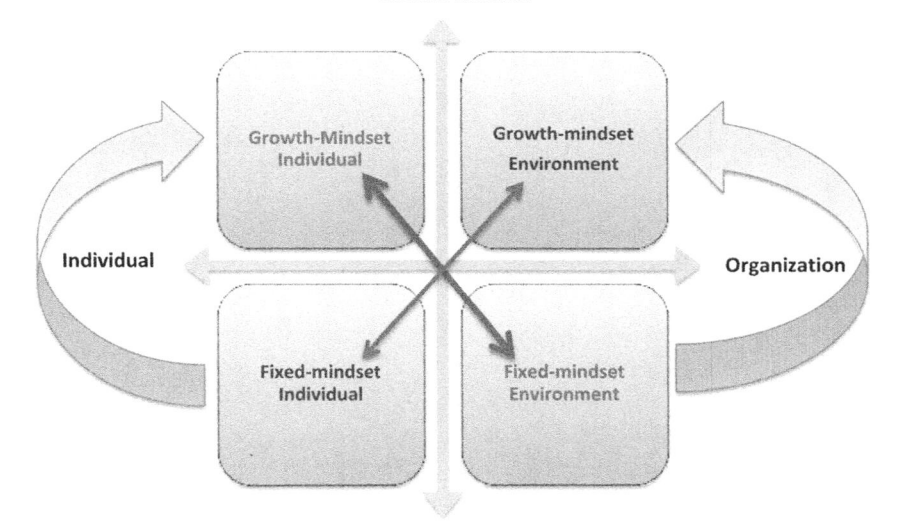

Growth Mindset

Growth-Mindset Individual	Growth-mindset Environment
Fixed-mindset Individual	Fixed-mindset Environment

Individual — **Organization**

Fixed-mindset

If a company wants to shift from a fixed-mindset to a more growth-mindset environment, it will be necessary to think about changing from a judgment- and validation-oriented approach to a more developmental approach. This is possible, but it requires deep change in policies, processes, identification- and selection models and tools. Changing processes and tools can be a long and expensive process, but if it is necessary to maintain competitive advantage in the long-run, it might be worth the effort.

Conclusion

FINDINGS

The aim of this research was to provide a comprehensive comparison of approaches used to identify high-potentials and go beyond the common definition: step up two levels within a time span of 2 to 5 years. Many organizations have chosen a different term for this talent category. They think that a high-potential category implies the existence of a low potential category, which wouldn't be fair nor equitable for the other employees. Findings show that 80 percent of the fifteen organizations approached have a high potential program, whereas Silzer and Church reported in 2008 one hundred percent. Results show that over 60 percent of these organizations avoid using the term high-potential. They replaced the term high-potential with 'rising talent', 'capacity to grow' population, 'best bets' or simply 'talents'. Of the remaining 40 percent who employ the term high-potentials, a few use it only for succession planning, while others employ it as a generic category. When the term high-potential is used within a succession planning context and refers to a specific target job, it is not employed as a generic label. Findings show

The Name of the Game

that high performance is 'a given' when assessing potential. Moreover, performance is measured against two scales, one that measures achievement and results, the other that measures behavior, attitudes and values. High-potentials are usually high performers that behave according to the values of the organization. Some companies spot their employees' performance against potential using the nine-box grid. More than fifty percent of the companies approached do not use this tool. They believe it isn't appropriate for the following reasons: some think it fosters an elitist approach to talent, others believe potential is too poorly defined and think promotability isn't the right focus, others find this tool too static. One company developed a 9 box grid that spots performance, in terms of achievements and results, against attitudes and behaviors. They use it to identify and visualize their key talent. In this organization behaviors and attitudes, that refer mostly to emotional intelligence qualities, are a precondition to career advancement.

There are two very different approaches to potential identification and assessment. The first assumes that potential can change over time (as well as company needs can change over time), therefore assessment and potential identification are an ongoing process that considers and reconsiders a possibly large talent pool; the second approach assumes that potential is a fixed quality, the tendency in this case is to have a restricted high-potential talent pool that will vary little over time. This second approach is commonly referred to as 'fishing in a pool of usual suspects'. Furthermore, findings show that companies that have restricted talent pools and go for a transparency policy, meaning that they tell formally high-potentials they are on the list, tend to keep recovery rates low, possibly beneath 1 percent. It makes sense, since communicating to a former high-potential he/she is not retained, is the kind of exercise nobody feels at ease with. Concerning the transparency policy, findings show that only 25 percent of the companies decided to communicate formally about who is on the list. Seventy five percent of the organizations do not tell formally who has been identified and selected. In some cases they give hints about who is identified, but they avoid giving any kind of confirmation. They don't want a high-potential category; they don't want to create a 'status' or a high-potential identity. A generic label would put the focus on validation. They judge this approach is too risky for the following reasons: it creates unnecessary expectations, it risks to demotivate many by creating a small and spoiled elite, and it can be the source of great frustration and a sense of helplessness for those who are not on the list anymore.

Many HR Directors report negative consequences when a transparency policy has been associated to a generic high-potential label. On the other hand, HR Directors who are in favor of communicating to high-potentials they are identified and selected have two main arguments to support their standpoint. The first is a motivational argument. It presupposes that knowing to be among the selected few increases motivation. The second, is a retention argument, meaning that if high-potentials know they are identified and selected, they will be more loyal to the organization, they won't consider external opportunities. I would like you to consider the following counter-arguments to these two standpoints:

- a high-potential is not supposed to need a label or external motivation to move forward;

- the second counter-argument is that if high-potentials are not given opportunities to learn, to grow and to stretch, there are no labels or status that should retain them; and if this is what motivates and retains them, then we should start having serious doubts about their potential.

The only valid condition for increasing motivation and retention is in short-term succession planning context or when the term high-potential is referred to a target job.

Some companies reported having up to twenty percent of high-potentials, others reported no more than 1,2% of total population. In average most reported having between 5 to 10% of high-potential population. There is no right or adequate percentage rate. Evaluating the best approach means always referring to the company's needs. However, when the talent pool becomes more and more restricted in terms of percentage of total population, when your recovery rates are crunched year after year and you decide to go for a transparency policy, you are now conscious of the implications of this choice.

SOME FINAL CONSIDERATIONS RELATED TO THEORY AND FINDINGS

Understanding implicit theories and their impact on our choices, decisions and the way we set goals is important when it comes to defining talent management policies and strategies. Implicit theories enable us to have a more profound understanding and consciousness of what moves us, since they provide a framework to guide our goals as individuals and they define the name of the game and its rules within organizations.

We saw that there are entity theorists (fixed-mindset) and incremental theorists (growth-mindset). The entity theorists believe that traits are firmly established and fairly consistent, it's all about 'have' and 'have nots'. If this is translated into an organizational perspective, it means that either you are a natural talent or you aren't. This perspective leads talent management policies and practices to be mainly focused on performance assessment, judgment, validation and ticking the competencies boxes. The focus will be set on experience and past performance, employees will be evaluated against their peers, and the tendency will be to fish in a pool of usual suspects. The smaller the talent pool, the more stable it is, if you communicate who is on the high-potential list, the higher the risk of creating a fixed-mindset environment. From a cognitive perspective entity theorists have to be good right now, they don't have the luxury of becoming. Therefore, they will be more focused on crystallized intelligence, consolidated knowledge and competencies.

The incremental theorists believe traits are always varying over time; they can be developed. They see traits as not having much predictive value, and, therefore, are not as confident to pass judgments. In this case, from an organizational perspective, talent management policies and practices will be more focused on development and learning. They will tend to value entrepreneurial spirit, calculated risk taking and future development options more than entity theorists. Growth-mindset people and organizations will be more focused on development also from a cognitive perspective; beyond past performance they will focus on transferable skills, on fluid intelligence.

Having an insight into the way people construct reality gives an insight into individual choices and behaviors as well as into an organization's culture and values. They are useful when it comes to defining what kind of potential we are looking for. The danger for entity theorists and fixed-mindset environments is that they could prevent employees from fully realizing their potential. These theories are different ways of constructing reality and have strong impact on our everyday choices and decisions. Identifying and assessing potential implies making choices and constructing the future reality of our organizations. The future reality of our organizations depends on whether we embrace a 'war for talent' perspective or not. The 'war for talent' perspective implies a fixed-mindset approach to talent. It means that talent is a limited resource and that people either have it or don't. If this is the assumption, then organizations have to go down in the trenches and fight for the few stars on the market. The fixed-mindset approach means creating an elitist culture. An elitist culture that communicates officially who are the high-potentials, means taking the risk of demotivating in average 95 percent of the population and creating 5 percent of potentially arrogant and fixed-mindset leaders. It also means creating unnecessary expectations that risk to be frustrated and lead to demotivation, and last but not least, it risks to create a sense of helplessness for those that find out they are not on the list anymore. Organizations need all their resources, hundred percent of their resource's engagement and motivation to achieve and maintain competitive advantage. Making the choice of promoting an elitist culture is something that can cost you dearly in the long run. I recommend to adopt a more mature and growth oriented approach to talent. HR executives as well as consultants should make an effort to create a developmental environment that focuses on progress and feedback, rather than on performance benchmarked against peers, validation and judgment. An effort should be made to assume a non-linear system perspective and try to understand how human behavior and organizational systems mutually influence each other. This approach might enable us to better understand the essence of particular situations and help us identifying virtuous behavioral patterns. The other option is to stick to a reassuring cause-effect linear system and it's illusionary predictive value. Thus, in case you use the 9-box-grid, use it as a visual aid, as a tool that gives you a picture of your talent pool at a given moment in time, and not for it's supposed predictive value. Since the 9-box-grid has no predictive value. When you praise your outstanding employees, praise them for specific actions. Avoid generic labels. And think of valuing collective effort by all means.

HR Directors face important responsibilities when defining talent management policies. The policies as well as the way they are applied give employees important cues about what the organization values. The findings supported by the theoretical background show that these choices have important implications, both on the organizational culture as on

The Name of the Game

employees' motivation. One hundred percent of organizations reported having a strong feedback culture, however feedback can be very different in its nature. Feedback helps us to know better our own strengths and weaknesses and learn from mistakes. A feedback session can be a sort of judgment, it can be a generic praise or a generic criticism that labels people; on the other hand it can be specific, focused on present and future competencies and be growth oriented. Shifting the focus from a person's 'promotability' to his/her 'future state of performance' means doing whatever is necessary to sustain learning and development in a feedback rich environment in the long term. A good start when assessing potential is to observe how a person reacts to setback. This will enable HR professional as well as managers to create the conditions for potential release. Giving feedback involves great responsibility, be it positive as well as negative feedback. Small linguistic cues have important implications on motivation, behavior and climate. Having consciousness of these theories can help making the right choices. If I was to give a single condensed recommendation it would be: praise specific actions; value collective effort[9].

---

9 See page 139.

Appendix 1
Interview Guide

1. Do you have a list of 'high potentials' in your company? If yes, since when (3 years, 5 years or more)?

2. Do you call them High-potentials? If you call them differently, why?

3. How do you define 'high potential'?

4. How many 'high potentials' are there? (% of total population/ number of individuals).

5. How do you identify and assess? What kind of process/ tools are applied?

6. When are they identified during their career? Do you have various evaluations at given stages? Are there career milestones?

7. If yes, are there particular differences in identifying and managing high potentials who are between 25-30 years old / 30-35 years old/35-40 years old/ 40-45 years old? (check diversity issues)

8. Do 'high potentials' receive special treatment compared to the non-high potentials?

9. Do you have within your company a defined HR process/ policy that concerns only this "high potential" (or key-talent) population?

10. What are the actions/practices of the different HR specialties (Compensation & Benefits, Talent Development, Career Management, Training, ….) that are involved and how?

11. Do you have a particular C&B policy for high-potentials? Give details…

12. If you have a high-potential population, do you think it is an equitable practice, is it just? (personal point of view) Please explain…..

13. Investment and return on investment on high potentials are measured? If yes, how?

14. Does the CEO / senior executives dedicate time to High potentials in your company?

15. Are 'high potentials' formally informed they are on the list? If yes, how?

16. Is it possible to be on the high potential list and then be ejected? If yes, how do you deal with those cases? How do you communicate?

17. What is the recovery rate of high potentials from one year to the next? (entry/exit from the HP list)

18. Do they have a defined career path and transparency on their next moves within the next 3-5 years? (greater responsibility, authority, greater scope...)

19. The notion of 'high potential' is it always strongly associated with strong leadership skills and management competencies? (check diversity issues)

20. If I tell you 'high potential' on-hold, is it a non-sense? (Diversity)

21. Is 'potential' inborn or acquired in your personal point of view? Explain why.

Bibliography

Adams, John S., "*Towards an Understanding of Inequity*", Journal of Abnormal and Social Psychology, n°67, November 1963, pp.422-436.

Adams, J.S., *Inequity in social exchange. Adv. Exp. Social Psychology*, 62, 1965, 335-343.

Bandura, Albert, *Social Foundations of Thoughts and Action*, Englewood Cliffs NJ, 1986.

Bandura, Albert, *Organizational Applications of Social Cognitive Theory*, Australian Journal of Management, December 1988.

Bar-On, Reuven, *Emotional Quotient Inventory: Technical Manual*, Toronto, MHS, 1997.

Beechler, S., Woodward, I.C., *The Global War for Talent,* Journal of International Management, 15, 2009, pp.273-285.

Biddle, Stuart et al., *Motivation for Physical Activity in Young People: Entity and Incremental Beliefs about Athletic Ability*", Journal of Sports Sciences 21, 2003, pp.973-989.

Blackwell, L., Dweck, Carol S., Trzensniewski K., *Implicit Theories of Intelligence Predict Achievement across an Adolescent*

Transition: A Longitudinal Study and an Intervention, Child Development 78, N°1, 2007, pp. 246-263.

Blaire, Clancy, *How similar are fluid cognition and general Intelligence? A developmental neuroscience perspective on fluid cognition as an aspect of human cognitive ability*, Behavioral and Brain Sciences, Vol.29, 2006, pp.109-160.

Boudreau, J.W. and Ramstad, P.M., *"Talentship, Talent Segmentation, and sustainability: A new HR decision science paradigm for a new strategy definition"*. In Human Resource Management, 44, 2005, pp.129-136.

Bower, B., *Reworking Intuition: Business Simulations spark rapid workplace renovations*, in Press Science News, October 2004.

Boyatzis, Richard and McKee, Annie, *Lessons of Experience*, The Free Press, 1988.

Boyatzis, R., *The competent Manager: A model for Effective Performance*, NY, John Wiley and Sons, 1982.

Brash, Joanna and Yee, Lareina, *Unlocking the full potential of women at work*, McKinsey & Company, Quarterly Review, May 2012.

Brewster, C., *Different Paradigms is HRM: questions raised by comparative research*. In P.Wright et al., Research in personnel and HRM (pp.213-238) Greenwich. CT Jay Press, 1999.

Buchanan, G., Seligman, M., *Explanatory Style and Achievement in School and Work*, Hillsdale NJ, Lawrence Erlbaum, 1995.

BIBLIOGRAPHY

Campell, M. Smith, R., *High-Potential Talent: A view from inside the Leadership Pipeline,* Center for Creative Leadership, in Press, 2010.

Cattell, Raymond B., *"Theory of Fluid and Crystallized Intelligence: a Critical Experiment"*, Journal of Educational Psychology, Vol 54; N°1, 1963, pp. 1-32.

Cerdin, Jean Luc and Bird, Allan, *Careers in a Global Context Global,* Revue Management & Avenir, 1, 2004.

Cerdin, Jean-Luc, *L'expatriation,* Paris, Ed. d'Organisation, 2002.

Cerdin, Jean-Luc, *Gérer les carrières,* Caen Ed. Management et Société, 2000.

Cerdin, Jean-Luc, *Expatriation,* Editions d'Organisation, 2ème Edition, 2002.

Collins, Jim, *Good to Great: why some companies make the leap…and others don't,* NY Harper Collins, 2001.

Collins, Jim, *How the mighty fall,* NY, HarperCollins, 2009.

Conway, Andrew R.A., Kane, Michael J., Engle, Randall W., *Working Memory capacity and its relation to general intelligence,* In Cognitive Sciences, Vol.7, N°12, December 2003, pp.547-482.

Corporate Leadership Council, *Realizing the Full Potential of Rising Talent (Vol.I and II),* Washington DC, Corporate Executive Board, 2005.

Cowan, N., *Working Memory Capacity*, NY, Psychology Press, 2005.

Cowan, N., *The magical number 4 in short-term memory: a reconsideration of mental storage capacity*, Behav.Brain Sc., 24, pp.87-185, 2001.

Coyle, Daniel, *The Talent Code*, Arrow Books 2010.

Crowe E. and Higgins E.T., *Regulatory Focus and Strategic Inclinations: Promotion and Prevention in Decision Making*, Organizational Behavior and Human Decision Processes, 69, 1997, pp.117-132.

Csikszentmihalyi, Mihalyi, *Flow: The Psychology of Optimal Experience*, NY, Harper and Row, 1990.

Davidson, O.B. and Eden, D., *Remedial self-fulfilling prophecy: Two field experiments to prevent Golem effects among disadvantaged women*, Journal of Applied Psychology, 85, 2000, pp.386-398.

Deci E.L., Nezlek, J., Sheinman, L., *Characteristics of the Re-warder and Intrinsic Motivation on the Rewardee*, Journal of Personality and Social Psychology 40, 1981, pp.1-10.

Dejoux, C., Ansiau, D., Wechtler, H., *Compétences Emotionnelles, capacités d'apprentissage des dirigeants : le cas d'une entreprise française de service*, Revue Internationale de Psychologie, Vol.12, n°8, 2006, pp. 165-189.

Dejoux, C., *GPEC et getion des Compétences*, Dunod, Coll. Topos, 2008.

Dejoux, C. and Thévenet, M., *Talent Management*, Dunod, 2012.

BIBLIOGRAPHY

Dominick, Peter G., Gabriel, Allison S., *Two sides of the Story: An interactionist Perspective on Identfying Potential,* Industrial and Organizational Psychology, 2, 2009, pp.430-433.

Duckworth A.L., Seligman, M.E.P., *Self-Discipline Outdoes IQ Predicting Academic Performance in Adolescents,* Psychological Science 16, 2005, pp.939-944.

Durgin, T.V., *Identifying the Learning Agile Leader,* in Press Loominger Human Capital Institute, June 2006.

Dweck, C.S. and Molden, D.C., *Self-theories: the construction of free will,* in J.Baer, JC. Kaufman, and R.F. Baumeister (eds), *Are we free? Psychology and free will,* NY, Oxford University Press, 2008.

Dweck, Carol S., *Self-theories: their role in motivation, personality, and development,* Philadelphia: Psychology Press, 1999.

Dweck, Carol S., *Mindset: how you can fulfill your potential,* NY, Random House, 2006.

Dweck, C.S., Mueller, C.M., *Praise for Intelligence Can Undermine Children's Motivation and Performance,* Journal of Personality and Social Psychology, 75, 1998, pp.33-52.

Dweck, C.S. and Elliot A., *The Handbook of Competence and Motivation,* NY Guilford Press, 2005.

Dweck, C.S., *Mindset: The new psychology of success,* Random House, 2006.

Dweck, Carole S.,Y.Hong, C.Chiu, D.Lin, and W.Wan, *Implicit Theories, attributions, and Coping: a Meaning System Approach,*

Journal of Personality and Social Psychology 77, 1999, pp.588-99.

Dweck C. S., Chiu C. and Hong, Y, *Implicit Theories: Elaboration and Extension of the Model*, Psychological Inquiry 6, 1995, pp.322-333.

Dweck, C.S., and Leggett, E.L.A., *A social cognitive approach to motivation and personality*, Psychological Review, 95, 1988, pp.256-273.

Dweck, C., *Beliefs that make smart people dumb.* In: Sternberg, R. (Ed.), *Why smart people can be so stupid.* Yale University Press, New Haven, CT, 2002.

Dweck, C.S. and Grand Halvorson H., *Clarifying Achievement Goals and Their Impact*, Journal of Personality and Social Psychology 85, N°3, 2003, pp.541-543.

Engel, R.W. and Kane M.J., *Executive attention, working memory capacity, and a two-factor theory of cognitive control*, In B.Ross ed., *The Psychology of Learning and Motivation*, NY Academic Press, 2004, pp. 145-199.

Evans, P., Lank, E & Farquhar, A., *Managing Human Resource Management in International Firms: Lessons from Practice*, In P.Evans, Y.Doz and A. Laurent (Eds) *Human Resource Management in International Firms.* Hampshire, MacMillan, 1989.

Evans, P., Pucik, V., & Barsoux, JL., *The Global Challenge: frameworks* for international Human Resource Management, London, McGraw-Hill, 2002.

BIBLIOGRAPHY

Fernandez-Araoz, Claudio, Groysberg, Boris, Nohria, Nitin, *How to hand on to Your High Potentials: Emerging best practices in manging our company's future leaders*, in Harvard Business Review, October 2011.

Fiedler, Fred E., "*When IQ + Experience ≠ Performance*", Leadership and Organizational Development Journal, 22/3, 2001, pp.132-138.

Flechl, Victoria, *Work-Life Balance: a comparative Study of Women in Senior Management Positions in Austria, UK and Denmark,*, 2009.

Föster, J., Grant Halvorson H., Idson L.C., and E.T. Higgins, *Success/Failure Feedback, Expectancies, and Approach/Avoidance Motivation: How regulatory Focus Moderates Classic Relations*, Journal of Experimental Social Psychology, 37, 2001, pp.253-260.

Feuerstein, R., Rand, Y., Jensen, M., & Tzriel, D., "*Prerequisites for assessment of learning potential : The LAPD model*", in C.S. Lidz, (ed.), *Dynamic assessment: an interactional approach to evaluating learning potential*, NY Guilford Press, 1987.

Galinsky, A.D., and Mussweiler T., *First Offers as Anchors: The role of Perspective- Taking and Negotiator Focus*, Journal of Personality and Social Psychology 81, 2001, pp. 657-69.

Gardner, Howard, *Extraordinary minds*, NY, Basic Books, 1997.

Geers, A., Wellman J., and Lassiter G, *Dispositional Optimism and Engagement: The Moderating Influence of Goal Prioritization,*

Journal of Personality and Social Psychology, 2009, pp.913-932.

Gladwell, Malcolm, *The Talent Myth*, The New Yorker, July 22, 2002.

Goleman, Daniel, *Emotional Intelligence: why it can matter more than IQ*, NY, Bantam, 1995.

Goleman,, Daniel, *Social Intelligence*, Random House, NY, 2006.

Goleman, Daniel, *Working with Emotional Intelligence*, Bantam Book, 2000.

Goleman, Daniel, *Leadership:the Power of Emotional Intelligence*, Bentam Book, 2002.

Goleman,D., Boyatzis, R., McKee A., *Primal Leadership:Realizing the Power of Emotional Intelligence*, Harvard Business School Press, 2002.

Good, Darren G., *Explorations of cognitive agility: a real time adaptive capacity*, PhD. Thesis submittend in partial fulfillment of the requirements, Department of Organizational Behavior, Case Western University, 2009 (unpublished).

Graen, G., *Early identification of future executives: a functional approach*, Industrial and Organizational Psychology, 2, 2009, pp. 437-441.

Grant Halvorson, Heidi, PhD., *Succeed: how we can reach our goals*, Penguin Group, NY, 2011.

BIBLIOGRAPHY

Gray, Jeremy, Chabris, Christopher F. and Braver, Todd S., *"Neural Mechanism of general Fluid Intelligence", in* Nature Neuroscience, vol.6, N°3, March 2003.

Gray, Jeremy, Thompson, Paul M., *Neurobiology of Intelligence: Science and Ethics.* Nature Reviews, Neuroscience, Nature Publishing Group,Vol 5, 2004, pp.471-81.

Groysberg, B., Nanda, A., Nohria, N., *The risky business of hiring stars.* Harvard Business Review, (May 1), 2004, pp.1-10.

Guilbert, D., *Stumbling on Happiness,* NY Knopf, 2006.

Hall, D.T., *"Carrers in and out of organizations",* Thousand Oaks CA Sage, 2002.

Hankin, Steven, *The war for Talent,* McKinsey &Company, 1997.

Henson, R.M., *Key Practices in Identifyng and Developing Potential,* Industrial and Organizational Psychology, 2, 2009, pp.416-419.

Heslin, Peter, Latham, Gary and VandeWalle, Don, *The effect of Implicit Person Theory on Performance Appraisals,* Journal of Applied Psychology 90, 2005, pp.842-856.

Heslin, Peter A., VandeWalle, Don and Latham Gary, *Keen to Help? Managers's IPT and their Subsequent Employee Coaching,* in Personnel Psychology 59, 2006, pp.871-902.

Heslin, P.A., *Potential in the Eye of the Beholder: The Role of Managers Who Spot Rising Stars,* Industrial and Organizational Psychology, 2, 2009, pp.420-424.

Hayman, Gail D., Dweck, Carol S., *Children's Thinking about Traits: Implications for Judgments of the Self and Others*, in Children Development 64, 1998, pp.391-403.

Janis, Irving, *Groupthink*, Boston, Houghton Mifflin 2nd Ed., 1982.

Jonides, John, *How does practice make us perfect?* Nature Publishing Group, 2004, pp.10-11.

Kane, M.J., & Engle, R.W., *Working memory Capacity and the control of attention: the contributions of goal neglect, response competition and task set to Stroop interference*, J.of Exp.Psychol. Gen. 132, pp. 47-70, 2003.

Kane, M.J. et al., '*For whom the Mind Wanders, and When : An Experience- Sampling Study of Working Memory and Executive Control in Daily Life*", Psychological Science, 18, 2007, pp.614-621.

Korn Ferry Institute (written by De Meuse, K.T., Dai G. and Hallenbeck G., *Using Learning Agility to identify High Potentials around the World*, 2009,

Korn Ferry/ Whitehead Mann publications, *Discover the DNA of Future CEOs*, Board and CEO Services, 2009.

Larkan, K., *Talent War: How to Find and Retain the Best People for your Company*, Marshall Cavendish Int., 2006.

Larkan, K., *Winning the Talent War: the 8 Essentials*, Marshall Cavendish, 2008.

BIBLIOGRAPHY

Lawler, E.E., *Talent: Making People your Competitive Advantage*, Jossey-Bass, 2008.

Lawler, E.E. and O'Toole, J., *The American Workplace*, NY, Plagrave macmillan, 2006.

LeDoux, Joseph, *The Emotional Brain: The Mysterious Underpinnings of Emotional Life*, NY, Simon & Schuster, 1996.

Lombardo Michael M., Eichinger, Robert W., "*High Potentials as High Learners*", in Human Resource Management, Vol. 39, N°4, 2000, pp.321-330.

Martocchio, Joseph J., *Effects of conceptions of Ability on Anxiety, Self-Efficacy, and Learning and training*", Journal of Applied Psychology 79, 1994, pp.819-825.

McClelland, David C., *Testing for competence rather than Intelligence*, American Psychologist 46, 1973.

McNatt, E., *Speaking of Memory: Eric Kandel discusses Freud's Legacy, memory's foibles and the potential of drugs that boost brainpower*, in Press Scientific American Mind, October 2008.

Mendenhall, Mark E., Macomber, James H., Gregersen, Hal and Cutright, Marc, "*Nonlinear Dynamics: A new perspective on IHRM Research and Practice in the 21st Century*", in Human Resource Management Review, Vol.8, N°1, 1998, pp.5-22.

McClelland, David C. et al., '*How do Self-Attributed and Implicit Motives Differ ?*", Psychological Review, Vol.96, N°4, 1989, pp.690-702.

The Name of the Game

McCall, Morgan W., *High Flyers: Developing the next generation of Leaders*, Boston Harvard Business School Press, 1998.

McKee Annie and Boyatzis, Richard, *Resonant Leadership*, Harvard Business School, 2005

McKee, Annie and Boyatzis Richard, *Primal Leadership*,

McLean, Bethany and Peter Elkind, *The Smartest Guy in the room: The amazing rise and scandalous fall of Enron*, NY, Penguin Group 2003.

Midgley, Dominic, "*Tales from the Talent War*", in Press, Director Publications, April 2011.

Michaels, E., Handfield-Jones, J., Axelrod, B., *The War for Talent*, Harvard Business Press 2001.

Miner, John B., *Organizational Behavior I: Essential Theorie of Motivation and Leadership*, ME Sharp, 2005.

Mone et al., Organizational Decline and Innovation: a contingency framework, *Academy of Management Review*, 23, 1, 1998, pp.115-132.

Nisbett, R., *Intelligence and How to Get It*, NY, WW.Norton, 2009.

Nohria, N., *The war for global talent.* Chief Executive Magazine 16, 1999.

Oberauer et al., *Working memory and Intelligence, Their correlations and their relations: Comment on Ackermann, Beier and Boyle (2005)*, Psychological Bulletin, vol.131, N°1, pp.61-65.

BIBLIOGRAPHY

Orpen, Christopher, *The Effect of Mentoring on Employees'Career Success*, Journal of Social Psychology, 135, 1995.

Peretti, J.M., *Tous Talentueux*, Eyrolles, Ed. d'Organisation, 2009.

Perrig, W.J., Hollenstein, M., Oelhafen, S., "*Can we Improve Fluid Intelligence with Training on Working Memory in Persons with Intellectual Disabilities?*", Journal of Cognitive Education and Psychology, Vol.8, N°2, 2009, pp.148-165.

Pink, Daniel H., *Drive :the surprising truth about what motivates us*, Penguin, NY, 2009.

Pink, Daniel H., A whole New Mind: why right brainers will rule the future, NY, Penguin, 2006

Rand, Kevin et al., *Hope, but not optimism, predicts academic performance of law students beyond previous academic achievement*, Journal of Research in Personality 45, 2011, pp.683-686.

Robins, Richard and Pal, Jennifer, *Implicit Self-Theories in the Academic Domain: implications for goal orientation, attributions, affect, and self-esteem change*", Self and Identity 1, 2002, pp.313-336.

Robinson, C., Fletters, R., Riester, D. and Bracco, A., *The Paradox of Potential: A suggestion for Guiding Talent Management in Organizations*, Industrial and Organizational Psychology, 2, 2009, pp.413-415.

Roger, A. and Boullet, D., *Talents et Potentiels*, in J.M. Peretti, (coord), *Tous Talentueux*, Eyrolles, Editions d'Organisation, 2009, pp.33-40.

Rogers, R.W. and Smith, A.B., *"Spotting Executive Potential and Future senior Leaders"*, in Press, Wiley Periodicals, 2004.

Ryan, R. and Deci E., *Self-Determination Theory and the Facilitation of Intrinsic Motivation, Social Development and Well-Being*, American Psychologist 55, 2000, pp.68-78.

Siegler, Robert S., *The other Alfred Binet*, Developmental Psychology 28, 1992, pp.179-190.

Silzer,R., Chruch, A.H., *The Pearls and Perils of Identifying Potential*, Industrial and Organizational Psychology, 2, 2009, pp.377-412.

Starck, R., Caye, J.M., Teichmann, C., *Creating People Advantage 2011 – Time to Act: HR Certainties in Uncertain Times*, The Boston Consulting Group, 2011.Thévenet, Maurice and Cécile Dejoux, *Talent Management*, Dunod, Paris 2012.

Stickgold, R., and Ellenbogen J.M., *Quiet! Sleeping Brain at Work*, in Scientific American Mind, 23, 2008.

Thévenet, Maurice, *Managers en temps de crise*, Eyrolles, 2009.

Thévenet, Maurice, *Des Etoile Brillantes ...aux étoiles filantes*, Eyrolles, Editions d'Organisation, 2008.

Thévenet, Maurice, *L'hyperbole des talents*, in J.M. Peretti, (coord) *Tous Talentueux*, Eyrolles, Editions d'Organisation, 2009, pp.419-425.

Thomas, David C. et al, *Development of the cultural intelligence assessment*, Advances in Global Leadership, Vol.7, 2012, pp.155-178.

BIBLIOGRAPHY

Vogel, Edward K. and Luck, Steven, J., *The capacity of Working Memory for features and conjunctions,* in Nature, Vol.390, November 1997.

Vogel, Edward K., McCollough, Andrew W.,& Machizawa, Maro G., *Neural Measures reveal Individual differences in controlling access to working memory,* Nature, 2005, pp.500-503.

Wood, Robert and Bandura, Albert, *Impact of Conception of Ability on Self-Regulatory Mechanisms and Complex Decision Making,* Journal of Personality and Social Psychology 56, 1989, pp.407-415.

Wunderer, Rolf, *Employees as "co-intrapreneurs" – a transformation concept,* Leadership & Organization Development Journal, 22/5, 2001, pp.193-211.

The Name of the Game

PRAISE SPECIFIC ACTIONS.
VALUE COLLECTIVE EFFORT.

Maurizio Cattelan, Punta di Dogana 2007.

Untitled. Anti-hero (anti-trophée). Beaux Arts Magazine 2012.

A wink to my son Daniel, who read my thoughts and found an interesting visual synthesis to this work.

Made in the USA
Monee, IL
30 May 2023